ARIZONA
HIGHWAYS

CAMPING
GUIDE

100 of the Best Campgrounds in Arizona

By Kelly Vaughn Kramer

Text: KELLY VAUGHN KRAMER
Photographs: *ARIZONA HIGHWAYS* CONTRIBUTORS AND STAFF
Designer: KEITH WHITNEY
Copy Editor: C. J. HUTCHINSON
Photo Editor: JEFF KIDA
Maps: KAREN MINOT

Library of Congress Control Number: 2012918868
ISBN 978-0-9845709-9-7
First printing, 2013. Printed in China.

Published by the Book Division of *Arizona Highways* magazine,
a monthly publication of the Arizona Department of Transportation,
2039 W. Lewis Avenue, Phoenix, Arizona 85009.
Telephone: 602-712-2200
Website: www.arizonahighways.com

Publisher: WIN HOLDEN
Editor: ROBERT STIEVE
Senior Editor/Books: RANDY SUMMERLIN
Managing Editor: KELLY VAUGHN KRAMER
Associate Editor: KATHY RITCHIE
Creative Director: BARBARA GLYNN DENNEY
Art Director: KEITH WHITNEY
Design Production Assistant: DIANA BENZEL-RICE
Photography Editor: JEFF KIDA
Production Director: MICHAEL BIANCHI
Production Assistant: ANNETTE PHARES

WARNING: Camping in Arizona, in a wide variety of environments, involves some
physical risk. Each camper should be aware of those risks. Weather can be a
factor, along with wildlife and each camper's physical condition and backcountry
knowledge. The author has attempted to provide accurate information about each
campground. Users of this guide are urged to obtain full information and skills to
camp safely. The author and publisher disclaim any liability for injury or other loss
or damage incurred while visiting or camping at any site mentioned in this book.

Cover: KP Cienega Campground 📷 PAUL MARKOW

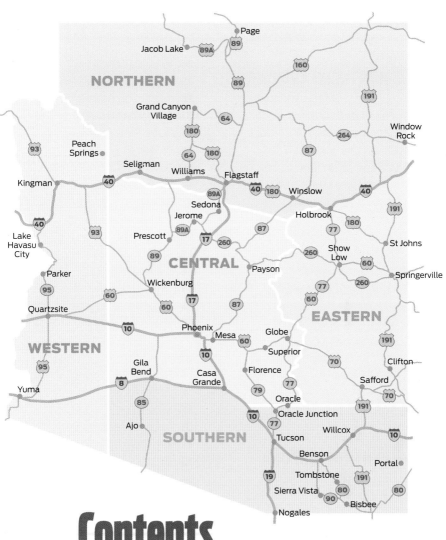

Contents

Contents

SOUTHERN ARIZONA

WESTERN ARIZONA

Preface

When I was 13, my mom and dad went to a sporting goods store, bought a tent, a Coleman stove and some sleeping bags and informed my sister and me that we were going to Oregon — to camp along the coast.

My sister, I think, was too young to be annoyed that we'd have to spend so much time in the car. I, on the other hand, wasn't looking forward to sitting in the back seat of our Dodge Caravan for days on end, so I buried my nose in a book, said, "Whatever," and off we went.

My nose stayed in that book and the one after it and the one after that. That is, until we reached Redwood National Park in Northern California. My dad drove the Dodge through a redwood. *Through a tree.* Sure, it was one of those touristy things that people do when they visit the park, but thus began my love affair with Mother Nature.

We wound our way out of California and into Oregon, visiting Sea Lion Caves and camping along some of the most beautiful coastline in the country. And while I did keep reading during downtime on the trip, I spent most of it bounding across rocks that peppered pretty creeks, breathing fresh air and marveling at the towering trees.

One late-summer day nearly two decades later, my husband, my son and I piled into our car and started driving. My daughter was with us, too, kicking me every time we drove on a particularly gravelly road. Although she didn't make her debut until five months later, I'm sure I'll tell her about the adventure one day.

During that trip, we ate a lot of Goldfish crackers, visited more than 30 campgrounds and spent a lot of time in the car — more peaceful, quiet, quality time than we could have reasonably expected from a boy who wasn't even 18 months old. Maybe it was the view from his back-seat window — plenty of ponderosa pines, aspens and blue sky — that kept

Kehl Springs is one of many campgrounds along the Mogollon Rim in Central Arizona. 📷 NICK BEREZENKO

him occupied. Maybe it was knowing that when we stopped somewhere, we'd unbuckle him and let him run.

As we journeyed home during a violent thunderstorm in the Upper Salt River Canyon, we spoke of how thrilled we were to have seen so much of Arizona.

That's the idea behind this book. Arizona isn't just a cactus-strewn desert. Sure, there's a reason that description prevails, but the state also has more than its fair share of gorgeous forests, lakes, streams and rivers. To experience them through camping is to experience them wholly.

Arizona Highways Camping Guide, which features 100 campgrounds organized by region, is for car campers, for people who are willing to load a bunch of gear into the backs of their cars or RVs, or into trailers and onto the backs of motorcycles, and head out for a weekend of adventure, whether solo, in small groups or in big ones. By no means is this a comprehensive guide to Arizona's campgrounds — if the book were to include every campground in the state, you wouldn't be able to lift it, let alone want to keep it in your car for easy reference. Some of the campgrounds that initially made my list didn't make the final cut. Some of them were difficult to reach; some were too primitive; and some were badly fire damaged. Undoubtedly, some of you will read this book and be disappointed that your favorite campground wasn't included. My hope is that the book inspires you to find a new favorite, or, at a minimum, another favorite.

I mentioned fire damage, and that's a topic worth discussing. While blazes caused by lightning strikes are Mother Nature's way of exercising her upper hand, fires caused by people are downright criminal. Take, for example, the Wallow Fire. It raged through the White Mountains during the summer of 2011 after two men abandoned a campfire they thought had been extinguished. Ultimately, it charred more than 530,000 acres, making it the largest wildfire in Arizona history. There were other fires that summer — Monument, Horseshoe 2 and a handful of smaller fires, as well. Humans caused the bulk of them.

As a camper, you are a steward of the land. It's your responsibility to leave your campsite as you found it, with every pine cone in place and every ash extinguished. That's one of the tenets of Leave No Trace, a set of principles you'll find outlined on page 21.

Some of the campgrounds in this book were, at one point or another, affected by fire. Some of the scars date back decades. Others are more recent. Ramsey Vista (page 136) and Reef Townsite (page 136) are good examples. The Monument Fire closed Carr Canyon Road for months, making Ramsey Vista and Reef Townsite inaccessible. In the months leading up to my deadline for this book, Forest Service officials worked to rebuild trails in the area, ensuring that people who once loved the long drive up Carr Canyon could still enjoy its recreational offerings.

A deer navigates fallen trees, victims of the Wallow Fire, which burned in the Apache-Sitgreaves National Forests during the summer of 2011. 📷 JACK DYKINGA

West Fork Campground (page 117) is another example. Wallow was bad, but it could have been even worse. Many of the recreation areas that closed during and immediately after the fire had reopened by press time, including West Fork. If you visit, you'll see burned trees and evidence of the fire's angry mosaic burn. But you'll also see new vegetation — aspens, wildflowers, grasses — that have emerged in the fire's wake. The White Mountains are open for business. Go. Hike, fish, cycle. Then camp along the Black River or at one of the other stunning campgrounds in the Apache-Sitgreaves National Forests.

Lockett Meadow was one of the campgrounds affected by the Schultz Fire, which burned near Flagstaff in 2010. While it didn't sustain direct fire damage, the campground was closed temporarily to undergo a safety assessment. Burned, fallen trees might have posed a hazard to campers, as could have loose rocks falling down burned hillsides.

I visited Lockett Meadow Campground (page 40) just a few weeks before the fire, on a day wrapped in a gorgeous blue sky. I had worked on a segment of the Arizona Trail with *Arizona Highways* Editor Robert

Lockett Meadow is one of the most scenic, popular campgrounds on the Coconino National Forest. 📷 TOM BEAN

Stieve and my husband, Nick. We cleared brush and rocks and defined boundaries as part of an Arizona Trail Day project. After, we drove along Schultz Pass Road and into the meadow. It was one of the most beautiful places I had visited during my research for this book, and I imagined the photograph that would accompany its entry. I don't think you'll be disappointed.

That afternoon, I sat in painter Bruce Aiken's studio, listening to him talk about his time in the Grand Canyon, entranced by some of the unfinished work on his easel. As I daydreamed, my dad called. My grandmother, who had long been sick, was dying. Within a few hours of my arrival back in Phoenix, she was gone.

My grandmother wasn't much of a camper, but I think she would have appreciated this book. She loved Arizona and spent many summers in

Flagstaff. I think of her when I think of Lockett Meadow, and I regret not having been able to take her on a road trip with me. That said, so many of my friends and family members buckled up for the long haul — Mom, Dad, Bobby, Rachel, Kat, thanks. Jenny, you owe me a trip, and you can bring the s'mores-making supplies.

No one logged more miles than my husband and children. Nick, I've never known a better navigator, and I thank you for not destroying the undercarriage of my truck during that trek to Indian Point. Jackson and Vera, I hope you'll hang on to this book when you're older. A sense of adventure will go a long way in your lives. Look at the trees, get lost in the sky, notice the way a river whispers — and always pack more Goldfish crackers than you think you'll need.

— *Kelly Vaughn Kramer*

Using This Guidebook

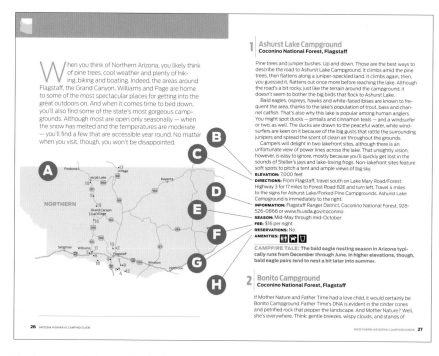

When you think of Northern Arizona, you likely think of pine trees, cool weather and plenty of hiking, biking and boating. Indeed, the areas around Flagstaff, the Grand Canyon, Williams and Page are home to some of the most spectacular places for getting into the great outdoors on. And when it comes time to bed down, you'll also find some of the state's most gorgeous campgrounds. Although most are open only seasonally — when the snow has melted and the temperatures are moderate — you'll find a few that are accessible year round. No matter when you visit, though, you won't be disappointed.

Pine trees and juniper bushes. Up and down. Those are the best ways to describe the road to Ashurst Lake Campground. It climbs amid the pine trees, then flattens along a juniper-speckled land. It climbs again, then, you guessed it, flattens out once more before reaching the lake. Although the road's a bit rocky, just like the terrain around the campground, it doesn't seem to bother the big birds that flock to Ashurst Lake.

Bald eagles, ospreys, hawks and white-faced ibises are known to frequent the area, thanks to the lake's population of trout, bass and channel catfish. That's also why this lake is popular among human anglers. You might spot ducks — pintails and cinnamon teals — and a windsurfer or two, as well. The ducks are drawn to the peaceful water, while windsurfers are keen on it because of the big gusts that rattle the surrounding junipers and spread the scent of clean air throughout the grounds.

Campers will delight in two lakefront sites, although there is an unfortunate view of power lines across the lake. That unsightly vision, however, is easy to ignore, mostly because you'll quickly get lost in the sounds of Steller's jays and lake-loving frogs. Non-lakefront sites feature soft spots to pitch a tent and ample views of big sky.
ELEVATION: 7,000 feet
DIRECTIONS: From Flagstaff, travel south on Lake Mary Road/Forest Highway 3 for 17 miles to Forest Road 82E and turn left. Travel 4 miles to the signs for Ashurst Lake/Forked Pine Campgrounds. Ashurst Lake Campground is immediately to the right.
INFORMATION: Flagstaff Ranger District, Coconino National Forest, 928-526-0866 or www.fs.usda.gov/coconino
SEASON: Mid-May through mid-October
FEE: $16 per night
RESERVATIONS: No
AMENITIES:

CAMPFIRE TALE: The bald eagle nesting season in Arizona typically runs from December through June. In higher elevations, though, bald eagle pairs tend to nest a bit later into summer.

2 Bonito Campground
Coconino National Forest, Flagstaff

If Mother Nature and Father Time had a love child, it would certainly be Bonito Campground. Father Time's DNA is evident in the cinder cones and petrified rock that pepper the landscape. And Mother Nature? Well, she's everywhere. Think: gentle breezes, wispy clouds, and stands of

Each entry in this book includes a campground description, a Campfire Tale (a fact about the campground or its region) and a guide. The guide offers quick references to important details about each campground, including the following:

A. MAPS
The maps in this book are intended as general references. For precise road information and routes, please refer to the directions included for each campground, as well as additional sources, like an *Arizona Atlas & Gazetteer*.

B. ELEVATION
The elevation listed for each campground refers to its highest point. This number is important because it will give you an idea as to what to expect in terms of temperature. Obviously, higher elevations will equate to lower temperatures, and vice versa. Plan accordingly, especially when it comes to packing clothing and sleeping bags.

C. DIRECTIONS
Driving directions are included for each campground. Mileages are approximate and, in some cases,

Central Arizona's Mogollon Rim plays host to a variety of campgrounds. ⬤ MOREY K. MILBRADT

roads may have more than one designation. Take, for example, Cady Road (Los Burros Campground, page 111). It's also known as Vernon Road and County Road 3140. So what does that mean for you? First, travel with a map. While we've double-checked these directions, it's good to have backup. Second, it's always a good idea to call a campground's governing body — usually the Forest Service or a state or county park — to check directions, road closures and general road conditions. Unless otherwise noted, the roads that lead to campgrounds in this book are accessible to all vehicles.

D. INFORMATION

Before you pack the entire family into the car for a road trip to a campground, it's important — as we suggest in item C, above — to check with your destination's governing agency. In most cases, that's the Forest Service, and we've included phone numbers and websites for specific ranger districts with each entry.

Sometimes, road closures, wildfires or acts of nature limit access to a campground. Forest rangers will have up-to-date information about what's open where, and they'll be able to answer any questions before you head out the door.

E. SEASON

With the exception of a few campgrounds in this book, most are only open during specific seasons. For example, in higher elevations such as the White Mountains, campgrounds are typically open from late spring to early fall — or, after snow melts and before it falls again. In some cases, campgrounds make a limited number of sites available for off-season camping. Always check with a campground's governing agency before planning a visit. While opening dates are usually spot-on, nature can throw a wrench into best-laid plans.

F. FEE

Nominal nightly fees are common at most campgrounds in this book,

and a few destinations don't require payment. We've listed the fees that were in place at the time of publication. Again, if you have questions regarding fees, contact the Forest Service or other responsible agency. Many campgrounds are hosted, and the concessionaires who operate the sites will collect payment. In some cases, a self-service pay station will greet you when you enter a campground. Be honest. Most fees collected from campgrounds are reinvested right into the site and used to add or update amenities.

G. RESERVATIONS

Most campgrounds are available on a first-come, first-served basis. Occasionally, though, reservations may be made. Unless otherwise noted, you may make a campground reservation through the federal system by calling 877-444-6777 or visiting www.recreation.gov.

H. AMENITIES

Even though you camp to experience the purity of the great outdoors, it's nice to have basic amenities when nature calls. We've included icons for the amenities available at each campground. They are the following:

Toilets: Most of the campgrounds have toilets. But few are flush toilets, like the ones you'll find at Fool Hollow Lake Campground (page 105). The majority are vault or pit toilets, meaning they're rustic. Respect the signs posted in restrooms.

Showers: Camping is, naturally, a gritty experience, and most campgrounds don't feature showers among their amenities. You'll find a few in this book that do, however, and this icon indicates that you'll be able to rinse off somewhere other than in a lake or a stream.

Pets: In most cases, the only pet you'll be taking to a campground is a dog. This icon indicates that a campground is Fido-friendly. That said, pets should be restrained to a leash at all times.

Water: If you're not traveling with your own stash of water, shame on you. It's a precious commodity here in Arizona and can be lifesaving if you end up stranded. Always travel with more than what you think you'll need. If you see this icon after a campground entry, it means potable water is available on-site.

RV Hookups: Not everyone prefers a camping experience to take place under a tent. Many of the campgrounds in this book are open to trailers and RVs up to a certain size. This icon indicates that RV hookups are available at some of the sites.

Many of the campgrounds in this guidebook are open to trailers and RVs. 📷 PAUL MARKOW

Introduction

WHAT TO TAKE

Preparing for a camping trip is similar in many ways to preparing for any other adventure. While you may want to travel lightly, it's always a good idea to pack more provisions than you think you'll need, especially when it comes to clothing, water and food.

Basic Equipment
- Map and road atlas
- Matches
- First-aid kit
- Pocketknife or multitool
- Sunscreen
- Water
- Extra clothing
- Compass
- Flashlight
- Tent
- Extra food
- Insect repellent
- Small shovel

Clothing Many of the campgrounds in this book are nestled at higher elevations. While they may be warm during the day, temperatures can plummet once the sun goes down. Pack multiple layers of clothing.

Weather can be tricky in Arizona, and rain and wind can come out of nowhere. Consider packing a windbreaker and a poncho. They don't take much room and can save your other layers if you get caught in a storm. Remember, you'll be a long way from a washer and dryer.

Food Whether you like baked beans, protein bars or cocktail weenies, you'll want to pack more food than you think necessary. Blown tires, unpredictable weather, misread directions and other uncertainties can result in spending more time in the wilderness than you intended. If you're camping, chances are you also might be hiking, boating, swimming or fishing — outdoors lovers do fit a certain mold — and those activities burn a lot of fuel. If you are a well-rounded adventurer, pack a combination of proteins and carbohydrates.

Campfires should be contained to fire pits and must always be completely extinguished. 📷 PETER SCHWEPKER

Water Although some campgrounds offer potable water, you don't want to travel anywhere in Arizona without it, especially when the mercury creeps into the 80s, 90s and 100s. Most Arizonans are used to carrying a bottle of water wherever they go, but when you're camping, it's prudent to take that bottle and then some. Figure roughly 1 gallon of water per person, per day, and more if you're camping at lower elevations.

Some of the campgrounds you'll read about here are situated along streams or near lakes or rivers. That doesn't necessarily mean you'll have drinking water at the ready. In dire circumstances, you can drink from the Black River or from a lake, but boil the water first, or, at the very least, filter it using a thin piece of cloth. Microorganisms can make you seriously ill, so to travel and camp with confidence, consider purchasing a portable water filtration system.

First Aid Think of all the things that can happen during a camping trip — burns, rolled ankles, cuts, scrapes, insect bites, sunburns — then pack accordingly. At a minimum, Band-Aids, antiseptic, tweezers and a comb are a must. Why the tweezers and comb? Cactus barbs can be a doozy, and these tools are usually effective at removing them from skin. Most retailers carry basic first-aid kits, and you can add to or subtract from them as necessary.

AT CAMP

Fee Payment At state parks and at other more developed campgrounds, a volunteer or a ranger will greet you as you pull in and request payment before you enter. At other campgrounds, you'll pick your site, then pay a visit to a camp host, who will collect your payment. Or, you'll be left to your own devices and asked to put payment into a locked box. No matter what, pay the required fee. Many campgrounds depend on that revenue for maintenance and development. Sure, in some cases, no one will be watching, but do the right thing to ensure a pleasant camping experience for you and future generations of campers.

Setting Up If you're lost in the wilderness, it's always a good idea to find shelter first, and even though you've gone into the wild for the purpose of sleeping there, you'll want to do the same thing. Set up your tent before you hike, swim, boat or otherwise recreate. That way, if a sudden rainstorm hits, you'll be prepared.

Campfires What you're reading is the second version of this book. Shortly after my original deadline, Arizona experienced the biggest fire in its history, Wallow. The fire exploded when two campers failed to completely extinguish their campfire. They left for a hike and returned to find the forest ablaze. Ultimately, Wallow burned more than 530,000 acres in the Apache-Sitgreaves National Forests — and it could have been prevented.

All campgrounds in this book feature fire pits and grills. Use them. And when it's time to leave, make sure your campfires are out — dead out. The Forest Service provides these guidelines:
- Allow wood to burn completely to ash.
- Pour water over the fire, dousing all embers.
- Stir campfire ashes and embers with a shovel.
- Scrape sticks and logs to remove any embers.
- Stir the ash pile to ensure that it is wet and cold to the touch.
- If you don't have water, use dirt, and mix it with embers until the pile is cool. Don't simply bury the fire; it may smolder and catch roots ablaze.

SAFETY

The backcountry is called the backcountry for a reason. It's remote. Therefore, take these safety factors into consideration:

The Border At many campgrounds in Southern Arizona, you'll see signs that warn of illegal immigrant activity. You may encounter a person or a group that has crossed the border and is on the way to another part of Arizona. More likely, though, you'll just see garbage left over from their travels through the campground. If

Hualapai Mountain Campground (page 149) is nestled at the base of Aspen Peak. 📷 ELIAS BUTLER

you do encounter individuals you believe to be illegal immigrants, do not approach them. Instead, contact local authorities or the camp host.

Flash Floods Flooding is prevalent in Arizona, especially during the monsoon season, from July through September. Camping in canyons and along washes is especially dangerous during the rainy season, as storms can roll in with little warning.

If you find yourself in a dangerous situation, get to higher elevation and look for the quickest exit from the canyon. Here's the bottom line: If you're caught in water — even if it's only knee-deep — you can die. A usually dry wash can flood in seconds, and the water can be fast-moving. Pay attention to your surroundings and the sky to avoid a potentially fatal situation.

What's more, many of the roads in this book are suitable for sedans — in most cases. Never attempt to cross a flooded road in a sedan or any other type of vehicle. Stupid-motorist laws exist for a reason. Don't become a statistic.

Lightning Lightning is a common phenomenon in Arizona, especially at higher elevations, such as along the Mogollon Rim (see the Eastern Arizona chapter, page 94). Lightning is most common during monsoon season, which, incidentally, falls during summer, just when people are gung-ho to head to higher elevations.

If you're caught outdoors when a storm is imminent, avoid exposed areas such as meadows and lakes. Do not stand near tall trees or other large objects. Of course, don't stand in water. If you are caught in a lightning storm, crouch as low as possible and keep your feet flat on the ground. If you have a backpack, put it on the ground, then crouch on top of it. The pack can help insulate you from a strike.

Even during the summer, temperatures at high elevations can drop. Prepare by packing layers of clothing. 📷 PETER SCHWEPKER

Hypothermia At the opposite end of the spectrum, hypothermia, when your body loses heat faster than it can produce it, is another risk when you're camping. At higher elevations, cold, stormy weather can roll in quickly. Now, chances are, you'll be right next to your car, and you can just head home if roads are passable. But, if you're stuck, be aware of the signs of hypothermia.

Dehydration and Heatstroke

Arizona is known for its dominant sunlight, and while it's good for vitamin D intake, it can also be dangerous. Drink plenty of water. Lounge in the shade. Wear sunscreen. Cool yourself with wet washcloths or clothing. Don't camp in the desert in the middle of July. These things seem obvious, but when the adrenaline starts pumping and you're game for adventure, your judgment can become impaired.

Symptoms of Hypothermia

- Shivering
- Fatigue
- Loss of coordination
- Incoherence
- Hallucinations
- Pale appearance
- Warming sensation
- Goose bumps
- Drowsiness

Pack layers, pack a blanket and steer clear of higher elevations during the snowy season.

Rattlesnakes You've heard the adage: Rattlesnakes are more afraid of you than you are of them. Typically, that's true, but encountering one is still scary. You'll find them under rocks, tucked into areas of dense brush, under logs and in places you just can't see.

If you encounter a rattlesnake, stay calm, take a wide berth, and move slowly past it. If you're bitten, sit still and stay calm. Adrenaline and panic will spread the venom faster through your body. Get to a hospital as quickly as possible, and if you have cold packs in your cooler, apply them to the wound in the meantime.

Wildlife Yogi Bear has a reputation for a reason — he loves stealing the picnic baskets of visitors to Jellystone Park. And while Yogi's antics are fictional, the black bears that roam Arizona are real and will attempt to steal your food. Use the bear-proof boxes provided at many of the campgrounds in this book. Seal your extra food and garbage tightly and don't leave leftovers out in the open. If you encounter a wild animal — bear or otherwise — keep your cool. Do not run. Back slowly away, and make yourself seem as big as possible. Make noise to scare the animal or animals away. If you're camping with man's best friend, just remember that pets can attract wild animals. Keep them close at all times. The same goes for children.

WILDERNESS ETHICS

Leave a place better than you found it. That's the bottom line. Generations before you have enjoyed the campgrounds in this book and maintained them so that you can enjoy them today. It's your job to protect them for future generations. Do so by following the seven principles of Leave No Trace.

Plan Ahead and Be Prepared
- Know the regulations and special concerns for the area you will visit.
- Prepare for extreme weather, hazards and emergencies.
- Schedule your trip to avoid times of high use.
- Visit in small groups when possible.
- Repackage food to minimize waste.

Travel and Camp on Durable Surfaces
- Durable surfaces include established campsites, rock, gravel, dry grasses or snow.
- Protect riparian areas by camping at least 200 feet from lakes and streams, unless you're in a developed area where specially designated sites are at water's edge.

Dispose of Waste Properly
- Pack it in, pack it out. Thoroughly inspect your campsite for trash or spilled food. Pack out all trash, including leftover food, from campgrounds where garbage bins are not available.
- Deposit solid human waste in holes dug 6 to 8 inches deep and at least 200 feet from water and trails. Cover and disguise the hole when finished.

Most campgrounds in this book feature dedicated restrooms, but if nature calls when you're en route, follow these rules.
- Pack out toilet paper and personal

Respect for wildlife, like this Coues deer, is one of the Leave No Trace principles.

While exploration of cultural artifacts is one of the joys of camping in Arizona, leave the artifacts untouched. ◘ DAVID MUENCH

hygiene products.
- To wash yourself or your dishes, carry water 200 feet away from streams or lakes and use small amounts of biodegradable soap.
- Scatter strained dishwater.

Leave What You Find
- Preserve the past. Examine but do not touch cultural or historic structures and artifacts.
- Leave rocks, plants and other natural objects as you find them.
- Avoid introducing or transporting nonnative species.
- Do not build structures or furniture or dig trenches.

Minimize Campfire Impacts
- Campfires can cause lasting impacts to the backcountry. Always use a lightweight stove for cooking and enjoy a candle lantern for light.
- Where fires are permitted, use established fire rings, fire pans or mound fires.
- Keep fires small. Only use sticks from the ground that can be broken by hand.
- Burn all wood and coals to ash, put out campfires completely and scatter the cooled ashes. COMPLETELY.
- Don't leave until you're positive that your fire has been extinguished. It takes hundreds of years for a forest to rebuild after a fire.

Respect Wildlife
- Observe wildlife from a distance. Do not follow or approach animals.
- Never feed animals. Feeding wildlife damages their health, alters natural behaviors and exposes them to predators and other dangers.
- Protect wildlife and your food by storing rations and trash securely. Control pets at all times, or leave them at home.
- Avoid wildlife during sensitive times such as mating, nesting and raising young or in winter.

Be Considerate of Other Visitors
- Respect other visitors and protect the quality of their experience.
- Be courteous.
- Observe quiet hours.

Source: Leave No Trace Center for Outdoor Ethics

Bonito Campground
SHANE McDERMOTT

NORTHERN ARIZONA
CAMPGROUNDS

W hen you think of Northern Arizona, you likely think of pine trees, cool weather and plenty of hiking, biking and boating. Indeed, the areas around Flagstaff, the Grand Canyon, Williams and Page are home to some of the most spectacular places for getting into the great outdoors. And when it comes time to bed down, you'll also find some of the state's most gorgeous campgrounds. Although most are open only seasonally — when the snow has melted and the temperatures are moderate — you'll find a few that are accessible year-round. No matter when you visit, though, you won't be disappointed.

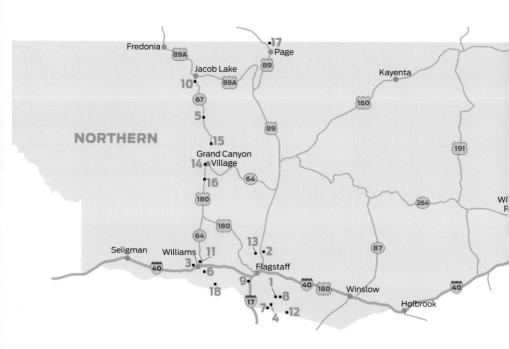

1 Ashurst Lake Campground
Coconino National Forest, Flagstaff

Pine trees and juniper bushes. Up and down. Those are the best ways to describe the road to Ashurst Lake Campground. It climbs amid the pine trees, then flattens along a juniper-speckled land. It climbs again, then, you guessed it, flattens out once more before reaching the lake. Although the road's a bit rocky, just like the terrain around the campground, it doesn't seem to bother the big birds that flock to Ashurst Lake.

Bald eagles, ospreys, hawks and white-faced ibises are known to frequent the area, thanks to the lake's population of trout, bass and channel catfish. That's also why this lake is popular among human anglers. You might spot ducks — pintails and cinnamon teals — and a windsurfer or two, as well. The ducks are drawn to the peaceful water, while windsurfers are keen on it because of the big gusts that rattle the surrounding junipers and spread the scent of clean air throughout the grounds.

Campers will delight in two lakefront sites, although there is an unfortunate view of power lines across the lake. That unsightly vision, however, is easy to ignore, mostly because you'll quickly get lost in the sounds of Steller's jays and lake-loving frogs. Non-lakefront sites feature soft spots to pitch a tent and ample views of big sky.

ELEVATION: 7,000 feet

DIRECTIONS: From Flagstaff, travel south on Lake Mary Road/Forest Highway 3 for 17 miles to Forest Road 82E and turn left. Travel 4 miles to the signs for Ashurst Lake/Forked Pine Campgrounds. Ashurst Lake Campground is immediately to the right.

INFORMATION: Flagstaff Ranger District, Coconino National Forest, 928-526-0866 or www.fs.usda.gov/coconino

SEASON: Mid-May through mid-October

FEE: $16 per night

RESERVATIONS: No

AMENITIES:

CAMPFIRE TALE: The bald eagle nesting season in Arizona typically runs from December through June. In higher elevations, though, bald eagle pairs tend to nest a bit later into summer.

2 Bonito Campground
Coconino National Forest, Flagstaff

If Mother Nature and Father Time had a love child, it would certainly be Bonito Campground. Father Time's DNA is evident in the cinder cones and petrified rock that pepper the landscape. And Mother Nature? Well, she's everywhere. Think: gentle breezes, wispy clouds, and stands of ponderosa pines that thrive despite the harsh soil.

These grounds are named for the Bonito lava flow, which oozed through more than 900 years ago. Slow and scalding, it covered everything, eventually cooling and forming the unique rocks and geologic features that characterize the landscape today. Sunset Crater National Monument is outside the campground, and is a must-visit.

The campground features pine-bough-covered sites and paved roads, as well as fire pits, grills and picnic tables. Ponderosa pines emerged from the volcanic landscape, creating shade and the unmatchable aroma of the outdoors. When it comes to making beautiful babies, Mother Nature and Father Time outdid themselves with Bonito.

ELEVATION: 6,900 feet

DIRECTIONS: From Flagstaff, travel northeast on U.S. Route 89 for about 12 miles to the turnoff for Sunset Crater/Wupatki (Forest Road 545), and turn right (east). Continue on FR 545 for about 2 miles to the campground.

INFORMATION: Flagstaff Ranger District, Coconino National Forest, 928-526-0866 or www.fs.usda.gov/coconino

SEASON: Mid-May through mid-October

FEE: $18 per night

RESERVATIONS: No

AMENITIES: 🚻 🐾 🗑

CAMPFIRE TALE: Wupatki National Monument is also near Bonito Campground. Built in phases in the 1100s, the pueblo features 100 rooms and was once home to about 125 people. For more information about the monument, visit www.nps.gov/wupa.

3 | Cataract Lake Campground
Kaibab National Forest, Williams

There are plenty of places to fish near the town of Williams — lakes abound — but Cataract Lake is one of the most popular. It's beautiful here, and the campground is no exception. That's because it's right along the water's edge.

Each of the 18 sites is set amid gorgeous green grass, and in spring, wildflowers peek from between the blades. Because sites are so close to the water, boats are popular at Cataract Lake. Remember, though, that they mustn't have horsepower greater than 10. Water recreation is the obvious draw at this campground (swimming, however, is prohibited), but if you prefer terrestrial endeavors, you won't be disappointed.

Ashurst Lake Campground, in the Coconino National Forest near Flagstaff, features two lakefront sites. 📷 SHANE McDERMOTT

An elk meanders through a marshy area of Mormon Lake, which is within walking distance of Dairy Springs Campground.  SHANE McDERMOTT

The ponderosa pines, the flowers and that brilliant green grass make Cataract Lake a nice place to sit back, relax and read a book. If you're visiting the campground during its off-season, you can picnic here, but you will have to make a short trek down the access road, which is closed to vehicles during winter.

ELEVATION: 6,800 feet

DIRECTIONS: From Interstate 40, east of Williams, exit at Cataract Lake Road and turn left. Take Cataract Lake Road to Cooper Road and turn right, following signs to the campground.

INFORMATION: Williams Ranger District, Kaibab National Forest, 928-635-5600 or www.fs.usda.gov/kaibab

SEASON: May through September

FEE: $14 per night

RESERVATIONS: No

AMENITIES:

CAMPFIRE TALE: The Grand Canyon is home to Cataract Canyon, which is better known as Havasu Canyon and well-known for its stunning waterfalls.

4 Dairy Springs Campground
Coconino National Forest, Flagstaff

If you're a hiker, this campground is for you. Three trails originate at Dairy Springs, including Ledges Trail, Dairy Springs Loop and Mormon Mountain Trail. They're all fairly simple day hikes, and all provide lovely views of Mormon Lake, which is just across the road.

The same views reign from the campground, where ponderosa pines and white firs are the stars of the show, providing nice cover for the countless birds that populate the area, hawks and harriers among them.

There is a group site at Dairy Springs, and it holds 40 people — just enough for a hootenanny, not enough for a hullabaloo.

Mormon Lake Lodge is within walking distance of the campground, so if you're hankering for a steak after hiking and don't feel like grilling on your own, you can head over there for some down-home cooking. Otherwise, you'll find fire pits, grills and picnic tables at each Dairy Springs site. After dinner, enjoy a ranger-led program in the amphitheater, or, if a bit of daylight is left, cruise around the self-guided nature trail.

ELEVATION: 7,000 feet

DIRECTIONS: From Flagstaff, travel south on Lake Mary Road/Forest Highway 3 for about 20.2 miles to Forest Road 90 and turn right. Continue on FR 90 for about 3.6 miles to Dairy Springs Road and turn right, following signs to the campground.

INFORMATION: Flagstaff Ranger District, Coconino National Forest, 928-526-0866 or www.fs.usda.gov/coconino

SEASON: May through mid-October

FEE: $16 per night (single site); $90 per night (group site)

RESERVATIONS: Yes

AMENITIES:

CAMPFIRE TALE: Dairy Springs Trail 136 is one of three trails that originate at Dairy Springs Campground. It winds through a forest of pines, firs and junipers at the base of Mormon Mountain and features interpretive stations along the way.

5 DeMotte Campground
Kaibab National Forest, North Rim, Grand Canyon

It's cold on the North Rim of the Grand Canyon, and at an elevation of 8,700 feet, DeMotte Campground can be chilly, too. That's why it doesn't open until mid-May, or later if seasonal snowfall has been heavy.

When the snow melts, this campground is worth a trip. Moderately sized with 38 campsites, DeMotte isn't too crowded. Pine trees and meadows make up the immediate scenery, and those meadows are

popular among wildlife — elk, squirrels, chipmunks and more.

While the meadows are something to marvel at, the campground is only 7 miles from the Canyon's North Rim. There, of course, you'll find some of the most spectacular scenery in the world. For adventurers, several hiking trails originate on the North Rim, including the North Kaibab Trail, which runs 14 miles into the Canyon, ending at the Colorado River and Bright Angel Campground. Back at DeMotte, you'll find picnic tables, fire pits and grills, and those will come in handy, for cooking out or staying warm.

ELEVATION: 8,700 feet

DIRECTIONS: From the North Rim entrance of Grand Canyon National Park, travel north on State Route 67 for about 7 miles to the campground.

INFORMATION: North Kaibab Ranger District, 928-643-7395 or www.fs.usda.gov/kaibab

SEASON: Mid-May through October

FEE: $17 per night

RESERVATIONS: No

AMENITIES: 🚻 🐴 🗑️

CAMPFIRE TALE: In 1872, Major John Wesley Powell named the park on the North Rim of the Grand Canyon for Harvey C. DeMotte, a mathematics professor from Wesleyan University who traveled with Powell's party during its Grand Canyon expedition.

6 Dogtown Lake Campground
Kaibab National Forest, Williams

Prairie dogs are social creatures. They live in "towns" that sometimes span hundreds of acres, burrowing and bounding across the landscape and munching on roots, seeds and grasses. And they're kind of cute.

The playful creatures were once abundant in the area near Dogtown Lake, which was named for the prairie dogs and their little town. Today, though, people far outnumber the little critters, particularly at Dogtown Lake Campground. Here, you'll find spring wildflowers, grassy meadows, pine trees and cool breezes. You'll also find the lake itself, which is popular among anglers, thanks to its population of trout and channel catfish.

The campground features an outdoor amphitheater, which is used for nature chats with forest rangers or by larger groups that have booked it for their own programs. It's also home to the Ponderosa Trail, which connects to Davenport Hill Trail. Davenport Hill Trail follows Dogtown Wash

Fog hovers over DeMotte Park, near DeMotte Campground on the Grand Canyon's North Rim. 📷 TOM BEAN

and climbs the hill itself for an elevation gain of about 800 feet, providing great views of the lake. If you're lucky, you might even spot a prairie dog or two. Slow down, prep your camera and prepare to watch them scamper.

ELEVATION: 7,000 feet

DIRECTIONS: From Williams, travel south on Fourth Street for about 4 miles to Forest Road 140 and turn left. Follow FR 140 for about 3 miles to Forest Road 132 and turn left. Follow FR 132 for about 1 mile to the campground.

INFORMATION: Williams Ranger District, Kaibab National Forest, 928-635-5600 or www.fs.usda.gov/kaibab

SEASON: Early May through early October

FEE: $18 per night (single site); $30 per night (double site); $210 per night (group site)

RESERVATIONS: Yes, for group site only

AMENITIES:

CAMPFIRE TALE: Prairie dogs have a high-pitched call that some say resembles a bark. Recent scientific studies have theorized that the animals have developed the most sophisticated animal language, using different sounds to identify different predators.

7 Double Springs Campground
Coconino National Forest, Flagstaff

Just down the road from Dairy Springs (page 31), Double Springs Campground feels like the larger campground's more introverted kid sister. There are 15 sites here, and they're more secluded than the sites at Dairy Springs. In other words, you won't feel as though you're right on top of your campground neighbor, being forced to make small talk.

Instead, you'll be too busy enjoying nature. The same kind of wildlife that frequents Dairy Springs is found here, including elk, deer, hawks and ospreys. The easy, 2-mile Lake View Trail begins at the campground. It climbs through ponderosa pines to a rocky outcrop that overlooks Mormon Lake, meadows and mountains.

The campground is stocked with fire pits, grills and picnic tables. Site 15 is nestled along a tiny creek, and although you might not hear it running, you will hear the breeze through the trees. What more could you ask for from a campground, really? Double Springs delivers.

ELEVATION: 7,000 feet

DIRECTIONS: From Flagstaff, travel south on Lake Mary Road/Forest Highway 3 for 20.2 miles to Forest Road 90 and turn right. Continue on FR 90 for about 4.8 miles to the campground.

INFORMATION: Flagstaff Ranger District, Coconino National Forest,

928-526-0866 or www.fs.usda.gov/coconino
SEASON: May through mid-October
FEE: $16 per night
RESERVATIONS: No
AMENITIES:

CAMPFIRE TALE: Double Springs is named for the twin springs at the campground. Pioneer rancher Les Hart is believed to have used the springs in the early 1900s.

8 | Forked Pine Campground
Coconino National Forest, Flagstaff

Situated on the opposite side of Ashurst Lake from Ashurst Lake Campground, Forked Pine is less congested, less rocky, a bit grassier and a whole lot more shaded. There are pine trees here — many of them — so it's safe to say the campground is appropriately named.

Windsurfing is a big draw for visitors, and the wind does seem stronger at this end of the lake. Pretty, lakefront sites mean you'll have great views of the windsurfers, as well as of Humphreys Peak.

The campground is stocked with standard amenities. Off-road motorized travel is prohibited, which means you won't hear much noise other than the wind through the trees, the lapping of the lake along its banks and the chattering of birds. Although the campground is officially open only from May through October, campers may use the sites off-season, as long as the road is open. None of the facilities is open when the campground is closed, though, with the exception of those near the main boat launch.

ELEVATION: 7,000 feet
DIRECTIONS: From Flagstaff, travel south on Lake Mary Road/Forest Highway 3 for 17 miles to Forest Road 82E and turn left. Follow the gravel FR 82E for 4 miles to the signs for Ashurst Lake/Forked Pine Campgrounds and turn left to Forked Pine.
INFORMATION: Flagstaff Ranger District, Coconino National Forest, 928-526-0866 or www.fs.usda.gov/coconino
SEASON: May through mid-October
FEE: $16 per night
RESERVATIONS: No
AMENITIES:

CAMPFIRE TALE: Windsurfing combines the elements of surfing and sailing. Surfers stand on a board 6 feet or longer while maneuvering a sail that varies in size depending on skill level. Windsurfing originated in Pennsylvania in 1948.

9 | Fort Tuthill County Park Campground
Fort Tuthill County Park, Flagstaff

If you think you see a pair of bears near the entrance to this campground, you're not the only person to have to do a double take. Because of its urban location, it's unlikely that Fort Tuthill Campground would actually host a bear. What you're looking at are the camp host's Newfoundland and Great Pyrenees dogs.

They're big, and so is this campground. Situated at Fort Tuthill County Park just south of Flagstaff, it features 90 individual sites, as well as space to accommodate RVs and trailers. The campground is part of the 413-acre county park, and because it features a fairground, picnic ramadas and an amphitheater, it's a popular place.

You won't feel alone at Fort Tuthill, but you will feel cool, thanks to the enormous pines that shade the campground. Also cool? The campground's proximity to Flagstaff, where, if you need a reprieve from the Great Outdoors, you'll find hip restaurants and shops.

ELEVATION: 7,000 feet

DIRECTIONS: From Flagstaff, travel south on Interstate 17 to Exit 337 and turn right. Follow signs to the campground.

INFORMATION: Coconino County Parks and Recreation Department, 928-774-3464 or www.coconino.az.gov/parks

SEASON: May through September

FEE: $16 per night; $20 for a site with a water hookup

RESERVATIONS: Yes, through the county: 928-679-8000

AMENITIES:

CAMPFIRE TALE: Fort Tuthill shares its name with a recreation area near Luke Air Force Base outside of Phoenix. There, military families can stay in cabins or yurts, or camp in their tents or RVs.

10 | Jacob Lake Campground
Kaibab National Forest, Fredonia

Jacob Lake was named for Mormon pioneer Jacob Hamblin, who settled in the area in the 19th century. If you saw a photograph of Hamblin, you might not be impressed by his pioneer looks, but you should be impressed by his reputation among the Indians with whom he dealt. You see, Hamblin was known as the "Buckskin Apostle."

Although Hamblin is long gone, the lake and campground that bear his

---

Jacob Lake Campground is popular among families, cyclists and boaters. 📷 SHANE McDERMOTT

Kaibab Lake Campground is one of the larger recreation sites on the Kaibab National Forest. 📷 SHANE McDERMOTT

name are fitting tributes. It's quiet here, north of the Grand Canyon, and sometimes the only sounds you'll hear are those of the wildlife, which includes elk, deer, and countless birds and squirrels.

The lake is open for fishing and boating, and the gorgeous, pine-tree-lined campground features standard amenities and spacious sites. If more adventure appeals to you, you're not far from the North Rim of the Grand Canyon, where hiking trails abound. Be sure, though, to obtain a backcountry permit if you plan to hike into the Canyon.

ELEVATION: 7,900 feet

DIRECTIONS: From Fredonia, travel south on U.S. Route 89A for about 30 miles to the campground, which is at the intersection of U.S. 89A and State Route 67.

INFORMATION: North Kaibab Ranger District, Kaibab National Forest, 928-643-7395 or www.fs.usda.gov/kaibab

SEASON: Mid-May through mid-August

FEE: $17 per night (single site); $70–$125 per night (group sites)

RESERVATIONS: Yes, for group sites only

AMENITIES: 🚻 🐕 🚰

CAMPFIRE TALE: You won't find the Kaibab squirrel many places, but you will find it near Jacob Lake. A native of the Kaibab Plateau, the squirrel is characterized by its black belly, white tail and tufted ears.

1 Kaibab Lake Campground
Kaibab National Forest, Williams

One of the larger campgrounds in the area, Kaibab Lake, just east of Williams, features a boat ramp, a huge group area, picnic tables, grills, an amphitheater where rangers host interpretive programs, and about a billion photo opportunities. The campground underwent a major renovation in 2011, and the many upgrades include a new camping loop, new pavement, new parking spurs and additional day-use parking, to name a few.

Anglers flock here for the brown trout, channel catfish, rainbow trout and brook trout. Don't try to swim around with the fish, however. It's not allowed, as the lake is a source of water for the town.

For a dose of history, it's easy to hop on Historic Route 66 from the campground. Of course, the Grand Canyon isn't far, either, and the adventure opportunities at the Seventh Natural Wonder are too many to list.

ELEVATION: 7,000 feet

DIRECTIONS: From Williams, travel east on Interstate 40 for 2 miles to Exit 165 for State Route 64 and turn right. Travel north on SR 64 for about 2 miles to the campground, which will be on your left.

INFORMATION: Williams Ranger District, Kaibab National Forest, 928-635-5600 or www.fs.usda.gov/kaibab

SEASON: Early May through early October

FEE: $18 per night (single site); $60–$382 (group sites)

RESERVATIONS: Yes, for group sites only

AMENITIES: 🚻 🏠 🚰

CAMPFIRE TALE: Known as "The Gateway to the Grand Canyon," Williams is at the base of Bill Williams Mountain. The town's main street is Historic Route 66.

2 Kinnikinick Campground
Coconino National Forest, Flagstaff

The road to Kinnikinick Campground might be considered hideous. That is, if you just can't stand the sight of lakes, pine trees and big sky. Although the drive gets a scenic A-plus — it meanders past Upper and Lower Lake Mary, Mormon Lake, Mud Lake and more — the real payoff is at the end of the journey, right on the banks of Kinnikinick Lake.

This popular trout-fishing destination makes for a stunning place to spend the night. Pine trees and juniper pepper a landscape that would otherwise be notable for wide-open spaces and, of course, the lake. Indeed, there's plenty of room to breathe here, especially if you snag one of the two lakefront campsites. You won't have to worry if you don't, though. The remaining sites offer big views of tree-covered hills and even a distant glimpse at Humphreys Peak.

Among the amenities are picnic tables, fire pits, grills and toilets. Plus, the camp host offers firewood for sale. If you brought your boat, feel free to use the launch. Otherwise, consider a walk near the Anderson Mesa Wildlife Protection Area at the junction of Forest Roads 125 and 82. Literally just up the road from the campground, Anderson Mesa is home to pronghorns, prairie dogs, elk, deer, mountain lions and waterfowl.

ELEVATION: 7,100 feet

DIRECTIONS: From Flagstaff, travel south on Lake Mary Road/Forest Highway 3 for 24.2 miles to Forest Road 125 and turn left. Follow the gravel road for 4.6 miles to Forest Road 82 and turn right. Follow the gravel road for 4.4 miles to the campground.

INFORMATION: Flagstaff Ranger District, Coconino National Forest, 928-526-0866 or www.fs.usda.gov/coconino

SEASON: May through September

FEE: $16 per night

RESERVATIONS: No

AMENITIES:

CAMPFIRE TALE: Kinnikinick Lake was likely named for the ancient Puebloan term *kinnik-kinnik*, which described the bearberry bushes that are prevalent in the area.

13 Lockett Meadow Campground
Coconino National Forest, Flagstaff

The clouds seem to hang low here, but maybe that's because the San Francisco Peaks loom so large. The peaks, the remains of a volcano, are just part of the scenic beauty at Lockett Meadow. The aspens will also awe you.

The campground is rustic, unhosted and one of the most charming in this book. It's set among the aspens, of course, and the 17 sites each offer spectacular views of the wilderness, including the ashy, cinder-cone landscape. In spring, the meadow plays host to wildflowers. In summer, the aspens blaze a brilliant green with new leaves. In fall, that foliage goes from green to gorgeous gold. Sites 7 and 8 are perhaps the most scenic, while 13 through 15 are nothing to scoff at, either. You won't find a bad site in the bunch.

If you're a well-rounded nature lover, the meadow offers access to the Inner Basin Trail, a 3.9-mile trek in the extinct caldera. It meanders along a primitive road, offering views of ancient lava flows. If you're lucky, you'll

In fall, Lockett Meadow's aspens turn a brilliant gold. 📷 SUZANNE MATHIA

also see one of the area's wild residents. Just as people are, porcupines, elk and black bears are drawn to Lockett Meadow.

ELEVATION: 8,600 feet

DIRECTIONS: From Flagstaff, travel northeast on U.S. Route 89 for about 12 miles to Forest Road 420 (directly across from the turnoff for Sunset Crater) and turn left. Follow FR 420 for about 0.5 miles to the turnoff for Forest Road 552 and turn right at the sign for Lockett Meadow. Continue on FR 552 for about 1.1 miles until you're forced to make a decision — turn right to Lockett Meadow or proceed to a dead end. Turn right, of course, and follow the road to the campground.

INFORMATION: Flagstaff Ranger District, Coconino National Forest, 928-527-3600 or www.fs.usda.gov/coconino

SEASON: June through mid-October

FEE: $12 per night

RESERVATIONS: No

AMENITIES:

CAMPFIRE TALE: Flagstaff was named for a flag-raising ceremony that occurred July 4, 1876. Settlers trimmed a pine tree and raised a flag in celebration of the nation's centennial.

4 Mather Campground
South Rim, Grand Canyon National Park

You won't find a landscape more spectacular than the Grand Canyon anywhere in Arizona. Anywhere in the world, perhaps. Carved over millions of years, its cliffs have long been the subject of photographers, essayists and regular joes who flock to marvel at its grandeur.

Luckily for those regular joes, there's Mather Campground. Situated in Grand Canyon Village on the South Rim, it offers tent and RV camping within walking distance of the village's general store. That makes for an easy, breezy camping experience, and that's a good thing because you'll be awfully busy when you're not in your tent.

If you can't find something to do at the Grand Canyon, you're just weird. From visiting Desert View Watchtower and Kolb Studio to wandering around El Tovar, you could while away days without leaving the Rim. If you do choose to venture into the Canyon on a hike, just remember to be prepared. In the case of the Canyon, what goes down must come up, so don't overestimate your hiking abilities. And no matter what you do, you won't want to forget your camera. This is, after all, a

Mather Campground is on the South Rim of the Grand Canyon, in Grand Canyon Village. ◘ PAUL MARKOW

natural wonder.

ELEVATION: 7,000

DIRECTIONS: Mather Campground is on the South Rim of the Grand Canyon, in Grand Canyon Village.

INFORMATION: Grand Canyon National Park, 928-638-7888 or www.nps.gov/grca

SEASON: Year-round

FEE: $18 per night

RESERVATIONS: Yes

AMENITIES:

CAMPFIRE TALE: Mather Campground and Mather Point were named for the first director of the National Park Service, Stephen P. Mather.

15 | North Rim Campground
North Rim, Grand Canyon National Park

Set among the aspens and pines on the North Rim of the Grand Canyon, this campground is, in a word, gorgeous. It's well loved by the rangers who care for it and the people who visit, and it shows. Shady, spacious sites are suited for families with tents, but RVs also have a place here.

In other words, there's plenty of room for everyone, and because the campground is right along the Rim, everyone should want to visit it. "But the North Rim is such a trek," you say. The amenities here make the trip worthwhile. In addition to flush toilets, coin-operated laundry machines and showers, you'll find a general store that contains just about anything you could need, from peanut butter to sweatshirts to gummy worms.

Just as at DeMotte Campground north of here, there's plenty to do on the North Rim, whether it's sitting back and soaking in the scenery or hiking into the Canyon. No matter your adventuring speed, you won't regret making the journey.

ELEVATION: 8,200 feet

DIRECTIONS: North Rim Campground is on the North Rim of Grand Canyon National Park.

INFORMATION: Grand Canyon National Park, 928-638-7888 or www.nps.gov/grca

SEASON: Mid-May through mid-October

FEE: $18–25 per night

RESERVATIONS: Required

Late-afternoon light kisses Wotans Throne, as seen from the Cape Royal overlook on the Grand Canyon's North Rim. ◘ MOREY K. MILBRADT

AMENITIES:

CAMPFIRE TALE: North Rim Campground is just south of the North Kaibab trailhead, the only maintained trail into the Grand Canyon from its North Rim. The trail runs 14 miles to its end at Bright Angel Campground and the Colorado River.

16 | Ten-X Campground
Kaibab National Forest, Tusayan

Sometimes, cups runneth over. Consider the campgrounds on the South Rim of the Grand Canyon those cups. When they runneth over, it's a good thing Ten-X Campground is there to help.

Just 4 miles south of the Grand Canyon's entrance, Ten-X is beautiful in its own right. You'll find a forest of pines and oaks, as well as 70 sites equipped with picnic tables, fire pits and grills. Because most of the hustle and bustle of this area is reserved for the Canyon, Ten-X seems quieter, which might be why so many birds, squirrels and chipmunks like it here.

And if you like birds, squirrels and chipmunks, you'll love the campground's self-guided nature trail. It's a great little jaunt for kids. Of course, if you're game for a bigger jaunt, the Grand Canyon is just a hop, skip and a jump up the road.

ELEVATION: 6,600 feet

DIRECTIONS: From Williams, travel north on State Route 64 for about 48 miles to the campground.

INFORMATION: Tusayan Ranger District, Kaibab National Forest, 928-638-2443 or www.fs.usda.gov/kaibab

SEASON: May through September

FEE: $10 per night

RESERVATIONS: Yes

AMENITIES:

CAMPFIRE TALE: *Tusayan* comes from the Spanish name for Black Mesa on the Hopi Reservation.

17 | Wahweap Campground
Lake Powell, Page

If campgrounds were to compete in a beauty pageant, the destinations around the Grand Canyon would likely take home the prize, as well as claim the first- and second-runner-up titles. That said, Wahweap Campground would be named Miss Congeniality. That's because it offers amazing views of Lake Powell.

North Rim Campground is tucked away along the Grand Canyon's North Rim. SHANE McDERMOTT

There are 112 tent and RV sites here, so you won't be alone with your views of the lake. Even though this campground is big, there isn't a site that's lacking in the pretty department. There is a standout, though — site 26. It sits on top of a hill that overlooks the bay. When the light plays off sandstone cliffs at sunrise and sunset, site 26 is a place you'll want to be.

In addition to amazing photo opportunities, you'll find plenty of amenities at Wahweap Campground, including showers, flush toilets and, in the tiny, friendly, lakeside town of Wahweap, all the supplies you might need.

ELEVATION: 3,800 feet

DIRECTIONS: From Page, travel north on U.S. Route 89 for about 5 miles to Wahweap Boulevard and turn right. Continue on Wahweap Boulevard for about 3 miles to the campground.

INFORMATION: Lake Powell Resorts & Marinas, 888-896-3829 or www.lakepowell.com

SEASON: Year-round

FEE: $23 per night

RESERVATIONS: Yes, through www.lakepowell.com

AMENITIES:

White Horse Lake Campground
Kaibab National Forest, Williams

If you're a fan of forests and fishing, this campground is for you. White Horse Lake is popular among anglers looking for trout and channel catfish, but it's also popular among people looking to escape into the outdoors.

Hiking and mountain-biking trails abound in the Kaibab National Forest, and plenty of natural and historical sites are within a short distance of White Horse Lake Campground, including Sycamore Point, J.D. Dam and the Overland Trail. And because the campground is so close to Williams, there are also plenty of things to do in town.

The campground is fairly large, with 94 single-unit sites. Each includes standard amenities — a picnic table, a fire pit and a grill — and 22 of them are wheelchair-accessible. While almost all campgrounds in this book are accessible to people who have disabilities, this one might have the largest number of wheelchair-friendly sites.

What's more, the campground has its own boat ramp, which makes lake access easy. While hosts can provide information and firewood, you'll have to be responsible for your own fishing gear.

ELEVATION: 6,600 feet

DIRECTIONS: From Williams, travel south on Fourth Street (Forest Road 173) for about 9 miles to Forest Road 110 and turn left. Follow FR 110 for about 7 miles to Forest Road 109 and turn left. Continue on FR 109 for about 3 miles to the campground.

INFORMATION: Williams Ranger District, Kaibab National Forest, 928-635-5600 or www.fs.usda.gov/kaibab

SEASON: May through early October

FEE: $18 per night

RESERVATIONS: Yes

AMENITIES:

Storm clouds build over Lake Powell, which plays host to Wahweap Campground. ◻ MOREY K. MILBRADT

Blue Ridge Reservoir
📷 NICK BEREZENKO

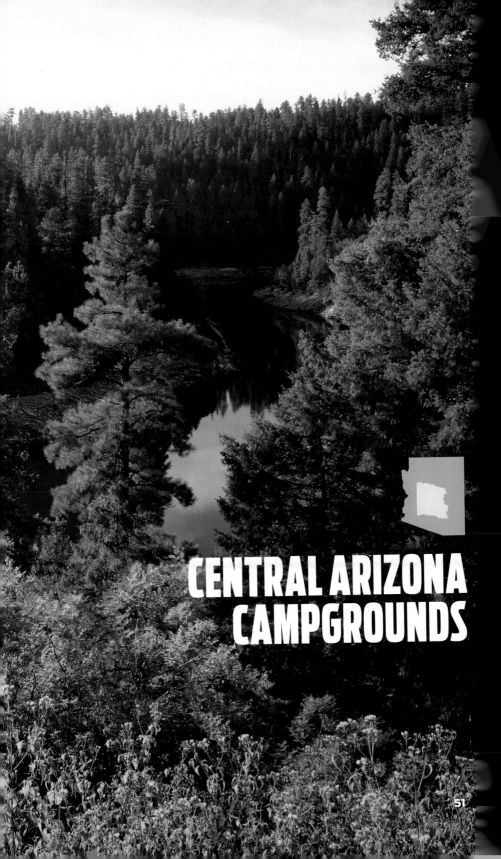

CENTRAL ARIZONA
CAMPGROUNDS

There's a reason this chapter features more campgrounds than any other section of this guidebook — they're easily accessible from anywhere in the state. From the Mogollon Rim to the Tonto National Forest near Globe and the red rocks of Sedona, there's some amazing beauty in this section of the state, and these campgrounds are some of the finest. What's more, many of them, particularly at the lower elevations outside of the Phoenix metro area, are open year-round, meaning that you and your family can hop in the car and camp in winter, spring, summer or fall.

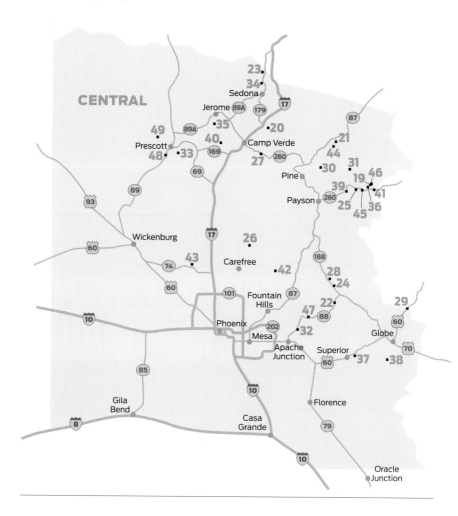

Aspen Campground
Apache-Sitgreaves National Forests, Heber

Situated at Woods Canyon Lake and along the Mogollon Rim, Aspen Campground is a water lover's dream. Boating, fishing, hiking, wildlife viewing — those are the most popular activities for people who want to take advantage of all the lake has to offer. But if you'd rather enjoy the standard camping activities — building s'mores, singing songs and sleeping under the stars — Aspen Campground is suitable for you, too.

As you can imagine, aspens make up the bulk of the scenery at this 136-site destination. You'll also find ponderosas, oaks and Douglas firs, along with enough squirrels, chirping birds and chattering chipmunks to provide backup vocals for your campfire songs.

Given Aspen's family friendliness, cool weather and proximity to the lake, sites fill up quickly. Reservations are available and recommended. For amenities, picnic tables, fire pits and grills are a given. Fulfilling your camping dreams is up to you.

ELEVATION: 7,600 feet

DIRECTIONS: From Payson, travel east on State Route 260 for 30 miles, and turn left at the sign for Woods Canyon Lake at Forest Road 300. Continue on FR 300 for 3.5 miles to additional signs for Woods Canyon Lake, and turn right. The campground is a mile down the road.

INFORMATION: Black Mesa Ranger District, Apache-Sitgreaves National Forests, 928-535-7300 or www.fs.usda.gov/asnf

SEASON: May through October

FEE: $18 per night

RESERVATIONS: Yes

AMENITIES:

CAMPFIRE TALE: Aspens grow in "clonal colonies," groups of genetically identical trees that sprout from a single seedling. One root system sustains the trees, whose leaves are known to quake and shiver, thanks to their flattened petioles (stalks).

Beaver Creek Campground
Coconino National Forest, Sedona

It's no wonder that people flock to Beaver Creek Campground. Nestled on the banks of Wet Beaver Creek, it's set in a sycamore-lined riparian area that backs against red-rock hills. Camping here is like camping in a postcard.

The road to the campground is nothing to scoff at, either. Manzanitas, piñon pines and junipers line Forest Road 618 as it crosses a one-lane bridge after about 1.4 miles, taking you over Red Tank Draw. From there, it turns to red dirt at 1.8 miles, then crosses another one-lane bridge after 2.3 miles before it leads to the campground.

Before you even reach its entrance, though, you might hear the buzz of cicadas, which are common here during summer — just like the campers who take advantage of the many amenities, including a free picnic area, fire rings and grills, and hiking, swimming and sightseeing opportunities.

This is a pretty place, all shady, shiny and scenic. What's more, it's environmentally conscious. Recycling bins are available throughout the campground.

ELEVATION: 3,800 feet

DIRECTIONS: From the junction of Interstate 17 and State Route 179, turn right on Forest Road 618 and travel about 2.3 miles to the campground, which will be on your left.

INFORMATION: Red Rock Ranger District, Coconino National Forest, 928-282-4119 or www.fs.usda.gov/coconino

SEASON: Year-round

FEE: $16 per night; $8 for a second vehicle

RESERVATIONS: No

AMENITIES: 🚻 🐕 🗑️

CAMPFIRE TALE: Bell Trail 13 and Apache Maid Trail 15 run through Wet Beaver Wilderness. Bell Trail is the only developed route into the wilderness area and winds along sandstone canyon walls and to Bell Crossing.

21 | Blue Ridge Campground
Coconino National Forest, Pine

You'll fall asleep on top of a car at Blue Ridge Campground. Seriously. Smashed, recycled cars compose the renovated sites here.

That's just one of the interesting facts about this destination, which is 5 miles north of Blue Ridge Reservoir (popular among water recreationists) along the Mogollon Rim. Other tidbits? Plenty of squirrels populate the campground, as do ponderosa pines. Fish are aplenty in the reservoir, making this a great camping destination for anglers. If you prefer hiking, trails are numerous. This is Rim Country, so no matter your recreational preference, you'll be able to do what you love while surrounded by some of Arizona's finest scenery.

Back at the campground, the $8 fee you'll pay to stay here does some good. Thanks to the Federal Lands Recreation Enhancement Act, the

Aspen Campground is along the Mogollon Rim, which stretches for approximately 200 miles and defines the southwestern edge of the Colorado Plateau. 📷 LAURENCE PARENT

Mogollon Ranger District uses 95 percent of the fees collected at Blue Ridge to maintain and improve the site, thus the recycled cars — and the awesome campground.

ELEVATION: 7,000 feet

DIRECTIONS: From Pine, travel about 30 miles north on State Route 87 to Forest Road 138 and turn right. Continue on FR 138 for about 1 mile to the campground.

INFORMATION: Mogollon Ranger District, Coconino National Forest, 928-477-2255 or www.fs.usda.gov/coconino

SEASON: Mid-May through September

FEE: $8 per night

RESERVATIONS: No

AMENITIES:

CAMPFIRE TALE: The recycled-car material used to renovate the site pads at Blue Ridge Campground is known as impact post, which is created by turning the smashed cars into a powder. The powder is then combined with gravel to create a durable, compacted surface.

22 | Burnt Corral Campground
Tonto National Forest, Apache Junction

Just 6 miles south of the spectacular Roosevelt Dam and along the waters of Apache Lake, Burnt Corral Campground doesn't live up to its name at all. That's because it's green and lush and surrounded by fantastic views of saguaro-studded mountains.

Many of the sites are right along the banks of the lake, including site 42, which is a great one if you can grab it. All sites feature standard amenities, and they're accessible by a paved road that winds through the campground.

In terms of recreation, the lake beckons boaters and anglers. For those who love to drive, the campground is right off the Apache Trail (State Route 88), a winding mountain road that was once a stagecoach trail. It climbs among saguaros, drops into surprising riparian areas, then climbs again as it approaches Roosevelt Dam, and it's something everyone in Arizona should experience at least once.

ELEVATION: 1,900 feet

DIRECTIONS: From Apache Junction, travel north on State Route 88 (the Apache Trail) for about 38 miles to the campground. The last 20 miles of SR 88 are an unpaved, one-lane gravel road. Alternatively, from the intersection of State Route 87 and State Route 188 south of Payson, travel east on SR 188 for about 33 miles to its junction with SR 88 and turn right. Continue on SR 88 for about 6 miles to the campground.

INFORMATION: Tonto Basin Ranger District, Tonto National Forest,

Many of the sites at Burnt Corral Campground are right along the banks of Apache Lake. 📷 DIANE DIETRICH LEIS

928-467-3200 or www.fs.usda.gov/tonto
SEASON: Year-round
FEE: A $6 Tonto Pass per vehicle is required.
RESERVATIONS: No
AMENITIES:

CAMPFIRE TALE: Construction on the Apache Trail began in 1919, when then-Governor George P. Hunt decided to build a transportation link between Phoenix and the mining hubs of Globe and Miami. There were several stops along the route, including Government Well, Mormon Flat, Tortilla Flat, Fish Creek and Snell's Station.

23 | Cave Springs Campground
Coconino National Forest, Sedona

Red Rock Country is recreation country, and as you make the drive from Sedona, along Oak Creek Canyon, to this campground, you'll realize that you're in the presence of like-minded individuals who just want to be outside. So, be prepared for a bit of traffic, especially on weekends. Relax, though. You're not in any hurry. Take a moment or 10 to soak in the

scenery, which includes the red rocks, as well as greenery. Think piñon pines, juniper and other scrub. As the road gains elevation, leafier trees and bigger pines come into view, and that fine foliage is exactly what you'll find at Cave Springs Campground.

Tucked along Oak Creek and shaded by tall, lanky pines and red-rock canyon walls, this campground is kid-friendly (Slide Rock State Park is minutes away), spacious and scenic. There's even a broad, green meadow that softens the view of the rugged canyon walls. Sites A15 and A21 are definite gems, backing right up to the creek. None of the sites is shabby, though, and all include picnic tables, grills and fire pits.

This is a great place to kick back and while away a weekend — especially after you've endured that traffic.

ELEVATION: 5,500 feet

DIRECTIONS: From the junction of State Routes 179 and 89A in Sedona, travel north on SR 89A for about 13 miles to the campground, which will be on your left.

INFORMATION: Red Rock Ranger District, Coconino National Forest, 928-282-4119 or www.fs.usda.gov/coconino

SEASON: Mid-March through Mid-October

FEE: $18 per night

RESERVATIONS: Yes

AMENITIES:

CAMPFIRE TALE: Slide Rock State Park was originally part of the Pendley Homestead, a 43-acre apple orchard in Oak Creek Canyon. Today, the park, which is named for the slippery creek bottom that runs adjacent to the homestead, is a prime destination for summer tourists.

24 | Cholla Recreation Site
Tonto National Forest, Fountain Hills

This is not a place for solitude. As the largest solar-powered campground in the United States, Cholla Recreation Site is big, popular and well developed. It features 206 sites in several loops that are, appropriately, named for chollas, such as the "Jumping Cholla" loop and the "Teddy Bear" loop.

You'll find families, RVs and gorgeous scenery, thanks to Roosevelt Lake and the surrounding mountains. You'll also find paved roads, playgrounds, picnic tables and ramadas at every site and solar-powered

Slide Rock State Park is a favorite among families and within minutes of Cave Springs Campground. ◘ DEREK VON BRIESEN

restrooms in each loop.

This campground is shadier than Indian Point (see page 64), so it's pleasant year-round. It's also within a few miles of several other recreation sites along the lake, including Orange Peel, Bermuda Flat and Bachelor Cove.

ELEVATION: 2,100 feet

DIRECTIONS: From Fountain Hills, travel north on State Route 87 (the Beeline Highway) for about 45 miles to State Route 188 and turn right. Follow SR 188 for 26 miles to the campground, which will be on your left.

INFORMATION: Tonto Basin Ranger District, Tonto National Forest, 928-467-3200 or www.fs.usda.gov/tonto

SEASON: Year-round

FEE: A $6 Tonto Pass per vehicle, per night is required.

RESERVATIONS: No

AMENITIES: 🚻 🐕 🗑️

CAMPFIRE TALE: Theodore Roosevelt Lake is the largest lake or reservoir situated entirely in Arizona, with the capacity to hold more than 1.65 million acre-feet of water. Former President Roosevelt dedicated the dam in March 1911.

25 | Christopher Creek Campground
Tonto National Forest, Payson

You'll pass Camp Tontozona on your way to Christopher Creek. That's where the Sun Devils of Arizona State University held their summer football camp from 1960 to 2007, then restarted the tradition in 2012. Back in the days of Coach Frank Kush, well, they might have been up in the ponderosa pines, but you can bet they were working their tushes off. At Christopher Creek, just the opposite is true. This is a place to kick back, breathe in crisp, fresh air and enjoy where you are, when you are.

Christopher Creek runs right through this campground, and you can fish for trout. But obey all warning signs. The creek is prone to flash flooding during storms. While anglers visit this campground because of its trout, so do bears, and you'll see warning signs to that effect.

Bears aside, Christopher Creek is one very green, very charming campground. Some sites are perched atop mini-stairs made of logs, and it's possible to camp right along the edge of the creek. Imagine falling asleep to the sound of the water and the whisper of wind through the pines. It's possible — as long as you don't invite Coach Kush.

Christopher Creek runs through its namesake campground and below the Mogollon Rim. 📷 NICK BEREZENKO

Autumn turns cottonwoods and sycamores along the Verde River, near Clear Creek Campground, shades of gold. 📷 NICK BEREZENKO

ELEVATION: 5,600 feet

DIRECTIONS: From Payson, travel east on State Route 260 for about 19 miles to the turnoff for Christopher Creek (Forest Road 159), which will be on your right. Follow the paved road past Christopher Creek Picnic Area to the campground.

INFORMATION: Payson Ranger District, Tonto National Forest, 928-474-7900 or www.fs.usda.gov/tonto

SEASON: April through October

FEE: $16 per night

RESERVATIONS: No

AMENITIES:

CAMPFIRE TALE: The hamlet of Christopher Creek lies 22 miles east of Payson, below the Mogollon Rim. And, according to the town's website, things are laid-back there: "Christopher Creek is for people who want to hear the wind in the high mountain forest, the rushing water of our pristine mountain streams or the bugle of a Rocky Mountain elk."

6 Civilian Conservation Corps Camp
Tonto National Forest, Carefree

While the young men of the Civilian Conservation Corps were busy build-ing the Cave Creek and Seven Springs recreation areas in the 1930s, they stayed at this campground, tucked along a quiet creek north of Carefree. The campground is accessible via Forest Road 24, which winds north through fire-damaged foothills. The Cave Creek Complex Fire, sparked by lightning, is to blame for the scorched trees and brush that line the road. The fire careened through 244,000 acres of forestland in June 2005.

While you will see remnants of the fire at the CCC Campground, its scars don't alter the site's charms. Although it is rustic — there are no amenities other than toilets, picnic tables and fire pits — sycamores and the creek create a pretty place to pitch a tent. The campground is adjacent to the trailhead for Cave Creek Trail 4, a 10.4-mile path through Sonoran Desert vegetation, as well as lush riparian areas.

ELEVATION: 3,500 feet

DIRECTIONS: From Carefree, travel north on Cave Creek Road (which turns into Forest Road 24) for about 17 miles to the campground.

INFORMATION: Cave Creek Ranger District, Tonto National Forest, 480-595-3300 or www.fs.usda.gov/tonto

SEASON: Year-round

FEE: A $6 Tonto Pass is required per vehicle, per night.

RESERVATIONS: No

AMENITIES:

CAMPFIRE TALE: In 1887, the Cave Creek Mistress Mine struck gold. But in 2005, when the Cave Creek Complex Fire tore through the Tonto National Forest north of Carefree, the mine — which had been a museum, gift shop, and bed and breakfast — was destroyed.

27 Clear Creek Campground
Coconino National Forest, Camp Verde

Just off State Route 260, this campground is nestled in a riparian area on the banks of Clear Creek. That means that sycamores and cottonwoods surround it — you know, the types of trees that thrive along water.

Although the creek is just a trickle through the campground, this is a popular destination on weekends. Maybe that's because of its proximity to Camp Verde or to Alcantara Vineyards. Most likely, it's because of its enormous picnic area and views of Verde Valley hills.

Reservations are required to use the group site. Because of the popu-larity of the site, and because it can accommodate 80 people, those res-ervations should be made as far in advance as possible.

If you're traveling with only a carful of people, though, you won't need reservations — just a camera, your camping gear and plans for a relaxing few days.

ELEVATION: 3,200 feet

DIRECTIONS: From the junction of Interstate 17 and State Route 260 in Camp Verde, travel east on SR 260 for about 8.4 miles to Forest Road 626 and turn left. The campground is about a half-mile down FR 626.

INFORMATION: Red Rock Ranger District, Coconino National Forest, 928-282-4119 or www.fs.usda.gov/coconino

SEASON: Year-round

FEES: $16 per night

RESERVATIONS: For the group site only

AMENITIES:

CAMPFIRE TALE: Situated just 12 miles east of Camp Verde, the West Clear Creek Wilderness is home to hiking trails, swimming holes and a rustic, primitive camping area near Bull Pen Ranch. Access the campground via Blodgett Basin Trail.

28 | Indian Point Recreation Site
Tonto National Forest, Fountain Hills

Nestled on the north shore of Roosevelt Lake, Indian Point is one of the smaller campgrounds in the area. But it's not the only thing you'll find on this side of the lake. If you're lucky, you'll spot a rare Southwestern willow flycatcher. Signs warn that some areas of the recreation area may be closed to protect the birds' nesting sites. Respect the closures but have your camera at the ready.

You'll need your lens at your campsite, too. The 54 sites at Indian Point fall within two separate loops, have great views of the water and come with grills and fire pits. Unlike most campgrounds in this book, Indian Point has no picnic tables. For campers with RVs, the Mogollon Loop is best; it has more room for large vehicles than the Anasazi Loop. You'll also find the boat ramp at Mogollon.

The Mazatzal Mountains loom in the distance, and don't be surprised to catch a smattering of bright yellow Mexican daisies and flashy purple salvia blooms during wildflower season. Small palo verdes and other desert scrub round out the list of foliage.

Although water recreation — fishing, boating and swimming — beckon campers to Indian Point during warmer months, this campground is short on shade, so it's best in cooler seasons.

ELEVATION: 2,200 feet

DIRECTIONS: From Fountain Hills, travel north on State Route 87 (the Beeline Highway) for about 45 miles to State Route 188 and turn right. Follow SR 188 for 20.3 miles to Forest Road 60/A-Cross. Turn left. Continue on FR 60 past Tonto Creek for 3.3 miles to Indian Point Recreation Site. Sites are scattered along the banks of the lake, which will be to your right. A high-clearance vehicle is recommended for crossing Tonto Creek. Do not cross when the creek is running.

INFORMATION: Tonto Basin Ranger District, Tonto National Forest, 928-467-3200 or www.fs.usda.gov/tonto

SEASON: Year-round

FEE: A $6 Tonto Pass is required per vehicle.

RESERVATIONS: No

AMENITIES:

CAMPFIRE TALE: The Southwestern willow flycatcher was placed on the federal endangered species list in 1995. The migratory bird is characterized by a grayish-green back and wings and a pale yellow belly.

9 | Jones Water Campground
Tonto National Forest, Globe

Jones Water Campground is for the birds. No, really. A variety of bird species nest here, and if your friends regularly confuse your binoculars for your eyeglasses, you should, too.

Bird-watching draws visitors to Jones Water, but so does the campground's isolated, primitive nature. It's a great place to hide away for a weekend. A rugged road leads to the campground, and while a high-clearance vehicle isn't required, one might be a good idea on this trip. Manzanitas, oaks, junipers and scrubby brush line the road, and as it climbs, you'll be treated to sweeping views of the mountains south of the campground.

With 12 sites, Jones Water is small, but the campsites are spacious and feature picnic tables, fire rings and grills. You'll need to BYOB, though. Bring your own binoculars, that is.

ELEVATION: 4,000 feet

DIRECTIONS: From Globe, travel 15.7 miles northeast on U.S. Route 60 to the campground, which will be on your right.

INFORMATION: Globe Ranger District, Tonto National Forest, 928-402-6200 or www.fs.usda.gov/tonto

SEASON: Year-round

FEE: None

RESERVATIONS: No

AMENITIES:

CAMPFIRE TALE: Miners founded Globe in 1875, and the tiny mountain town was a popular stop along the Arizona Eastern Railway. Today, one of Globe's most visited tourist destinations is Besh Ba Gowah Archaeological Park, which pays tribute to the area's Salado Indian history.

30 | Kehl Springs Campground
Coconino National Forest, Pine

A cruise along Forest Road 300 might have you thinking you've fallen asleep and woken up in the Pacific Northwest. Stands of pines — piñon and ponderosas alike — are seated in beds of stunning bright green ferns. This is the Mogollon Rim at its finest, and as you approach Kehl Springs Campground, the road tops out in meadowlike surroundings, with amazing views of Rim Country.

Everything around this rustic, eight-site campground is emerald-colored and clean. It's like Oz, only without the Lollipop Guild. There are, however, off-roading trails, so don't be surprised to see an ATV buzzing through the greenery.

Where the off-roaders aren't, the dandelions are, and photo opportunities abound. Kehl Springs Campground is near hiking trails that originate off of FR 300, including the easy General Crook Trail 130, which runs 25 miles along the Rim. While it's unlikely you'll tackle all 25 miles during your visit, you should at least attempt a few of them. Hiking along the Mogollon Rim is one of the great outdoors experiences that Arizona offers.

ELEVATION: 7,500 feet

DIRECTIONS: From Pine, travel north on State Route 87 for 13.6 miles to its junction with FR 300, also known as Rim Road, and turn right. Bear left at the fork of FR 300 and Forest Road 281 and travel 6.7 miles to the campground. FR 281 is pot-holed and gravelly in places, but generally well maintained and passable by sedan.

INFORMATION: Mogollon Rim Ranger District, Coconino National Forest, 928-477-2255 or www.fs.usda.gov/coconino

SEASON: Late-May through September

FEE: None

RESERVATIONS: No

AMENITIES:

CAMPFIRE TALE: From Kehl Springs Campground, you can see the Four Peaks in the Mazatzal Mountains range, as well as the Sierra

---

Kehl Springs Campground is flanked by pine trees and surrounded by wildflower meadows. PAUL GILL

Ancha, which fall between Roosevelt Lake to the south, Pleasant Valley to the north, Cherry Creek to the east and Tonto Basin to the west.

31 | Knoll Lake Campground
Coconino National Forest, Pine

Be prepared to stop as you wind along Forest Road 300 toward Knoll Lake — not because the road is poorly maintained or because of stop-and-go traffic, but because you won't be able to resist the photo opportunities on each side. To your right, you'll find the Mogollon Rim, gaping, green and gorgeous. To your left, you'll see pine trees, grasses and a whole lot of sky. In some areas, evidence of fire — felled and burned-out trees — provides a stark contrast to the bright green ferns growing at their bases. This is the juxtaposition of Mother Nature's cruelty and kindness.

You'll also pass a monument to the Battle of Big Dry Wash, an 1882 skirmish between White Mountain Apaches and the 6th Cavalry, after the Apaches fled their reservation and attacked ranches in the area.

A cattle guard marks the entrance to the campground, but don't be surprised to see people camping outside its boundary. That's allowed in this section of forest.

The 33 sites inside include fire pits, grills and picnic tables, and ponderosa pines provide shade to park your vehicle. Few sites have direct views of the lake for which the campground is named, but Knoll Lake is just a jaunt down the road. A small fishing lake full of trout, it's also popular among casual kayakers (motorized boats are prohibited).

ELEVATION: 7,400 feet

DIRECTIONS: From Pine, travel north on State Route 87 for 13.6 miles to its junction with FR 300, also known as Rim Road, and turn right. Bear left at the fork of FR 300 and Forest Road 281 and travel 22.8 miles to Forest Road 295E and turn left. Follow FR 295E for 3.4 miles to the campsite.

INFORMATION: Mogollon Rim Ranger District, Coconino National Forest, 928-477-2255 or www.fs.usda.gov/coconino

SEASON: May through October

FEE: $14 per night

RESERVATIONS: No

AMENITIES:

CAMPFIRE TALE: The Battle of Big Dry Wash was the last Army-versus-Apache battle in Arizona. The historic marker on your way to Knoll Lake Campground is 7 miles south of the actual battle site.

Knoll Lake derived its name from the tiny, pine-covered island at its center. 📷 NICK BEREZENKO

32 | Lost Dutchman Campground
Lost Dutchman State Park, Apache Junction

It's highly unlikely you'll find gold when you visit Lost Dutchman Campground, so don't set your expectations too high. That said, the campground will exceed every expectation you might have. Tucked inside the park, which is itself tucked amid the Superstition Mountains, the campground has 72 sites, including some designated for RVs.

Here, recreation rules, and it's possible to take an easy hike along the Treasure Loop or a far more strenuous trek along the Siphon Draw Trail, which leads to the top of Flatiron Rock. Ranger-led interpretive programs can occupy the kiddos, while wildlife watching will keep anyone occupied — javelina, hawks and mule deer are known to frequent the park.

Amenities also abound, including showers, which will come in handy after a long day on the trail. And that earns Lost Dutchman a gold star.

ELEVATION: 2,000 feet

DIRECTIONS: From the intersection of U.S. Route 60 and Idaho Road in Apache Junction, travel north on Idaho Road for about 2 miles to State Route 88 (the Apache Trail) and veer right. Follow SR 88 for about 5 miles to Lost Dutchman State Park.

INFORMATION: Lost Dutchman State Park, 480-982-4485 or www.azstateparks.com/parks/lodu

SEASON: Year-round

FEES: $15 per night, plus a $7 park-entrance fee

RESERVATIONS: Yes, 520-586-2283

AMENITIES:

CAMPFIRE TALE: In the 1870s, Jacob Waltz presumably found the remnants of the Peralta Gold Mine, which was abandoned in 1848 after Apaches killed most of the Peralta clan. Waltz is said to have hidden the gold somewhere in the Superstitions, and hopeful gold diggers have gone in search of it ever since.

33 | Lynx Lake Campground
Prescott National Forest, Prescott

Situated 15 minutes from downtown Prescott, Lynx Lake Campground may be an urban escape, but from the moment you enter the campground, you'll feel as though you're a million miles away. That's mostly because the campground is home to junipers, pines and manzanitas, as well as large

Lupine and Mexican goldpoppies bloom in Lost Dutchman State Park following rain-heavy winters. 📷 JEFF SNYDER

campsites — they're designed for five people but could easily fit 10.

Look up, and you'll see big sky, unobstructed by buildings or anything man-made. Lynx Lake, a half-mile down the road, is man-made but stocked with trout. It's a perfect place to waste a little time fishing, boating or hanging out and watching the wildlife, which includes great blue herons, ospreys, javelina and deer.

Trails, picnic areas and ramadas are plentiful, and individual sites are stocked with the standard grills and fire rings. If you're not keen on cooking your own camp meals, you won't have to travel far to find great food at one of Prescott's many restaurants.

ELEVATION: 5,500 feet

DIRECTIONS: From State Route 69 east of Prescott, turn right (south) onto Walker Road. Continue for 2.3 miles to the campground.

INFORMATION: Bradshaw Ranger District, Prescott National Forest, 928-443-8000 or www.fs.usda.gov/prescott

SEASON: April through October

FEE: $18 per night

RESERVATIONS: No

AMENITIES:

CAMPFIRE TALE: Sections of Trail 111 and Trail 94 near Lynx Lake are closed between December 1 and June 30 every year in an effort to protect nesting bald eagles.

Manzanita Campground
Coconino National Forest, Sedona

It isn't easy to stay at Manzanita Campground — not because it's hard to get to or because bears have taken over the grounds, but because it's small, creekside and very, very popular.

Amid the ash and box elders along Oak Creek, Manzanita features 18 sites that fill up early on weekends, thanks to families that love to splash around and fish in the water. It's so beautiful that you might be tempted to stay awhile.

If you do decide to leave the campground during your stay — and that's a big "if" — there's no shortage of things to do, from slipping and sliding around Slide Rock State Park to hiking down the trails in the Sedona and Oak Creek areas to swimming at Grasshopper Point. Just hurry back. You wouldn't want anyone to claim your site.

ELEVATION: 4,800 feet

Oak Creek runs along Manzanita Campground, nourishing a variety of grasses and trees. 📷 ELIAS BUTLER

DIRECTIONS: From the junction of State Routes 179 and 89A in Sedona, travel north on SR 89A for about 6.2 miles to the campground, which will be on your left. The turnoff for the campground comes quickly and without much notice. Pay attention to your odometer, and you shouldn't have any trouble. Otherwise, you'll be looking for a place to turn around, which isn't easy on the two-lane road.

INFORMATION: Red Rock Ranger District, Coconino National Forest, 928-282-4119 or www.fs.usda.gov/coconino

SEASON: Year-round

FEE: $18 per night

RESERVATIONS: Yes, for sites 9 through 19 only. Reservations must be made at least two days in advance.

AMENITIES: 🚻 🐾 🗑

CAMPFIRE TALE: The literal translation of the Spanish *manzanita* is "little apple," but no apples fall from the shrub. Characterized by red bark and twisted, gnarly branches, manzanita is common in Arizona, and there are 106 species of the plant worldwide.

35 | Mingus Mountain Campground
Prescott National Forest, Prescott

Mingus Mountain Campground is — where else? — near the top of Mingus Mountain. The drive to the top of the Prescott-area landmark is stunning and, in relation to other forest drives, it's a cakewalk.

With sweeping views of Sedona and the Verde Valley, and its big, shady sites, you might consider Mingus Mountain the epitome of the Great Outdoors. And you wouldn't be wrong. There's plenty to do, from lounging in a wildflower meadow or beneath a grove of pines to hiking one of four trails that are accessible from the campground to taking a day trip into Prescott or Jerome.

To capture those amazing Verde Valley views, sites 5 and 27 are your best bets. There are no scenic losers at the campground, though. When it comes to mountain camping, Mingus Mountain takes the cake.

ELEVATION: 7,500 feet

DIRECTIONS: From Prescott, travel north on State Route 89 to State Route 89A and turn right. Continue on SR 89A for about 19 miles to Forest Road 104 and turn right. Follow FR 104 for about 4 miles to the campground.

INFORMATION: Bradshaw Ranger District, Prescott National Forest, 928-443-8000 or www.fs.usda.gov/prescott

---

Mingus Mountain Campground rewards visitors with sweeping views of the Verde Valley. 📷 MOREY K. MILBRADT

SEASON: May through October
FEE: $10 per night
RESERVATIONS: No
AMENITIES:

CAMPFIRE TALE: In the 1880s, Jacob and Joseph Mingus opened a sawmill at the base of the mountain that now bears their name. At 7,726 feet, Mingus Mountain is the highest point in the Black Hills mountain range.

6 | Mogollon Campground
Apache-Sitgreaves National Forests, Payson

Whoever named Mogollon Campground shouldn't get credit for creativity. Situated on the Mogollon Rim, off of Forest Road 300, the name was a gimme. That said, whoever decided to put a campground here should get some serious kudos.

It's no secret that the Rim is gorgeous, or that pine trees make for stellar scenery. But Mogollon Campground is also just 2 miles from Woods Canyon Lake, where boating and fishing are the activities du jour, along with picnicking, wildlife watching and meandering along the interpretive nature trail. If a more intense hiking experience is more your speed, Rim Lake Vista Trail 622 originates a half-mile from the campground, and the moderate, 3.5-mile trek wanders right along the Rim.

Back at your campsite, you'll find grills and picnic tables, as well as garbage facilities, which don't exist at all campgrounds in this region. Mogollon Campground can accommodate trailers and motorhomes up to 32 feet in length at its 26 family sites, which are spacious. Although some of the sites in the campground's inner circle are prone to flooding during a big storm, sites 16 through 18 are some of the prettiest, nestled under a grove of immature pines.

ELEVATION: 7,500 feet
DIRECTIONS: From Payson, travel east on State Route 260 for about 30 miles to Forest Road 300, directly across from the ranger station, and turn left. Follow FR 300 for 3.9 miles to the campground, which will be on your left.
INFORMATION: Black Mesa Ranger District, Apache-Sitgreaves National Forests, 928-535-7300 or www.fs.usda.gov/asnf
SEASON: May through October
FEE: $14 per night
RESERVATIONS: No

Mogollon Campground is just 2 miles from Woods Canyon Lake, one of the most popular destinations on the Mogollon Rim. 📷 MOREY K. MILBRADT

AMENITIES:

37 | Oak Flat Campground
Tonto National Forest, Superior

Devil's Canyon. It takes a certain type of person to venture into a place with such a name — an adventurous person, a person who eats hikes along interpretive nature trails for breakfast. That's the type of person you'll likely find at Oak Flat Campground.

Known for its proximity to Devil's Canyon, Oak Flat is the prime destination for climbers and bouldering enthusiasts. But if you're a regular, run-of-the-mill, recreational camper, don't be discouraged. This is a great place for you, too.

Oak Flat is along the Gila-Pinal Scenic Route, which equates to plenty of photo opportunities. What's more, there are no fees, so the campground is popular on weekends. You'll want to arrive early for a better chance of securing a site. Big, burly oak trees shade the 16 campsites and plentiful picnic tables. Chances are, Devil's Canyon will make you hungry, so make good use of them.

ELEVATION: 3,900 feet

DIRECTIONS: From Superior, travel east on U.S. Route 60 for about 3 miles to Forest Road 469 and turn right. Continue on FR 469 for about 1 mile to the campground, which will be on your left.

INFORMATION: Globe Ranger District, Tonto National Forest, 928-402-6200 or www.fs.usda.gov/tonto

SEASON: Year-round

FEE: None

RESERVATIONS: No

AMENITIES:

CAMPFIRE TALE: Many who venture into Devil's Canyon do so to reach the famous Five Pools, some of the largest plunge pools in Arizona. Getting there requires serious climbing, rappelling, route finding, hiking and swimming. The trek can take seven to 11 hours, according to the American Canyoneering Academy.

Oak Flat Campground is popular among climbers because of its unique rock formations. 📷 ELIAS BUTLER

Pioneer Pass Campground
Tonto National Forest, Globe

Though Pioneer Pass Campground is a hop, skip and a jump from Oak Flat, a visit here requires a different type of adventurer — one who can stomach the lengthy, winding drive up Icehouse Canyon Road, especially if said adventurer is relegated to the back seat to entertain the children. Although the road is challenging, it has a payoff.

Tucked into the cool Pinal Mountains, Pioneer Pass Campground features broad mountain views and primitive camping. The 23 sites are scattered among big, yellow-bellied ponderosa pines, and you'll find a few grills and fire pits, as well as access to Pioneer (Squaw Springs) Trail and East Mountain Trail.

Hiking aside, it's the pine trees and the coolness that will draw you here. Just buckle your seat belt, sit back and enjoy the ride.

ELEVATION: 5,900 feet

DIRECTIONS: From Globe, follow the signs to Besh-Ba-Gowah Pueblo Ruins. Just past the turnoff, turn right onto Icehouse Canyon Road and continue 1.7 miles to the intersection of Forest Road 112 and Forest Road 55. Veer left onto FR 112 and continue 6.9 miles to Pioneer Pass Recreation Area.

INFORMATION: Globe Ranger District, Tonto National Forest, 928-402-6200 or www.fs.usda.gov/tonto

SEASON: May through November

FEE: None

RESERVATIONS: No

AMENITIES:

CAMPFIRE TALE: Members of the Civilian Conservation Corps constructed Pioneer Pass Recreation Area in the 1930s. Many of the trails that run through it are destined for Pinal Peak, the highest point in the Pinal Mountains at roughly 7,800 feet.

Ponderosa Campground
Tonto National Forest, Payson

State Route 260, which leads to Ponderosa Campground, is fairly slow moving, with speed limits around 45 mph in most places. That said, it's not terrible to look at all the junipers and scrubby piñon pines that line the road. Electrified elk crossings warn of the ungulates that populate

---

The Pinal Mountains are among a series of Sky Islands, high-elevation regions surrounded by desert, in Arizona. ◻ MOREY K. MILBRADT

the area, then the speed pops back up to 65 mph. About 10.5 miles down the highway, you'll pass a pretty meadow where cows graze, and immediately after, you'll enter the lush pine forest that characterizes the Mogollon Rim.

The aptly named Ponderosa Campground — yellowbellies are everywhere — smells of pine needles and campfire. What else would you expect at a site like this? There are open spaces for kids to wander around or toss footballs, and enough room for trailers. If you're camping in a tent, each site has a soft, well-cleared area to pop it. This is a relaxing, family-oriented campground, and it's possible to hang a hammock between two trees. The Abert Nature Trail runs along the perimeter of the campground. Enjoy it with the interpretive brochure, and watch for elk.

ELEVATION: 4,600 feet

DIRECTIONS: From Payson, travel east on State Route 260 for about 13 miles to the campground, which will be on your right.

INFORMATION: Payson Ranger District, Tonto National Forest, 928-474-7900 or www.fs.usda.gov/tonto

SEASON: Mid-April through October

FEE: $16 per night

RESERVATIONS: Yes

AMENITIES:

CAMPFIRE TALE: The National Register of Big Trees lists ponderosa pines with heights up to 227 feet. In January 2011, scientists measured a ponderosa pine in Oregon's Rogue River-Siskiyou National Forest at 268.35 feet.

40 | Powell Springs Campground
Prescott National Forest, Camp Verde

The road to this campground is primitive. Be prepared for navigating loose rocks and divots, and never attempt to travel the road when conditions are wet. You'll see a lot of low scrub and bouldered hills as you make your way to Powell Springs, and the road is part of the Great Western Trail.

During the dry summer months, it's unlikely that the creek for which this campground is named will be running, but that doesn't mean the site is any less charming. After about 2.8 miles, the road turns to pavement and begins winding as it climbs. Just over a hill, pine trees pop up, seemingly out of nowhere, and you'll sense that you're getting close to the campground, which you are.

The pines are a scenic staple at Powell Springs, as is manzanita. The small sites are well shaded and equipped with picnic tables, fire rings and grills, but this is a very basic campground — there are no drinking water, special amenities or services available. For well-traveled, road-rugged travelers, though, Powell Springs is a great escape that isn't too far from the civilization that lies just up the road in Camp Verde.

ELEVATION: 5,300 feet

DIRECTIONS: From the junction of Interstate 17 and State Route 169 south of Camp Verde, travel west on SR 169 for 5.3 miles to Cherry Creek Road (Forest Road 372) and turn right. Continue on the gravel road for 4.3 miles to the campground, which will be on your left, on Forest Road 372A.

INFORMATION: Verde Ranger District, Prescott National Forest, 928-567-4121 or www.fs.usda.gov/prescott

SEASON: Year-round

FEE: None

RESERVATIONS: No

AMENITIES:

CAMPFIRE TALE: The Great Western Trail runs 4,455 miles through Arizona, Utah, Idaho, Wyoming and Montana, linking 18 national forests. In 2000, the White House and U.S. Department of Transportation designated the Great Western Trail one of 16 National Millennium Trails.

41 | Rim Campground
Apache-Sitgreaves National Forests, Payson

Rim Campground is a little edgy. Not in the sense that you have to rock tattoos and a shaggy haircut to stay here, but in the sense that it's situated right along the Mogollon Rim. Although this campground is small, it's big on charm.

That charm is mostly because of the sight and scent of the pine trees that surround the campground like pretty girls surround a rock star. You won't be too close to your neighbors, thanks to spacious sites and distance between them. There are also a few spots where kids can scamper without worrying about disturbing campers who've traveled to the Rim for a little peace and quiet.

Really, that's what reigns here — peace and quiet — and sweeping, 100-mile views from the Rim itself. So while Rim Campground may be the backup to the campground at Woods Canyon Lake, she still rocks.

ELEVATION: 7,450 feet

DIRECTIONS: From Payson, travel east on State Route 260 for about 30 miles to Forest Road 300. Follow FR 300 for less than a mile to the campground, which will be on your left.

INFORMATION: Black Mesa Ranger District, Apache-Sitgreaves National Forests, 928-535-7300 or www.fs.usda.gov/asnf

Spring wildflowers bloom on a hillside overlooking Bartlett Lake, home to Riverside Campground. 📷 TOM BEAN

SEASON: Mid-May through mid-September
FEE: $14 per night
RESERVATIONS: No
AMENITIES:

CAMPFIRE TALE: Once known as Merzville, the tiny, unincorporated hamlet of Forest Lakes is 7 miles east of Rim Campground. There, you'll find gas and groceries, as well as a rich mining history, thanks to the area's abundance of manganese.

42 Riverside Campground
Tonto National Forest, Carefree

If you're a fan of Neil Young, a certain song might pop into mind as you're heading to this campground near Bartlett Lake in the Tonto National Forest. And though you will be "down by the river," the Verde River, the real highlight of this campground is its view of Bartlett Dam.

You'll first notice the dam as you round a corner on the road to the campground. You might even say to your travel companion: "Hey!

There's the dam!" But then as you round another bend, you'll see the dam in its enormous, breathtaking entirety: "No, that's the dam!" It's impressive, to say the least, and the 12-site campground is as well.

It's nestled at the base of saguaro-and-boulder-spotted hillsides, and sites are near enough to the river that you can dip your toes in it. Of course, you can also take advantage of all the recreational activities at the lake — the campground is near the Jojoba Boating Site.

ELEVATION: 1,600 feet

DIRECTIONS: From Carefree, travel east on Cave Creek Road for about 7 miles to Bartlett Dam Road and veer right. Continue for about 13 miles to the Jojoba Boating Site, and turn right onto Forest Road 19. Follow FR 19 for about 3 miles to the campground.

INFORMATION: Cave Creek Ranger District, Tonto National Forest, 480-595-3300 or www.fs.usda.gov/tonto

SEASON: Year-round

FEE: A $6 Tonto Pass is required per vehicle, per night.

RESERVATIONS: No

AMENITIES:

CAMPFIRE TALE: Engineers constructed Bartlett Dam between 1936 and 1939, using 182,000 cubic yards of concrete. The result was a 178,490 acre-foot reservoir, Bartlett Lake. The dam measures 308.5 feet high.

.3 | Roadrunner Campground
Lake Pleasant Regional Park, Phoenix

The history of Lake Pleasant Regional Park, just outside of Phoenix, can be traced to, well, prehistory. Archaeologists unearthed five ancient Hohokam sites during a survey of the area: a defensive site, a stone workshop, a farmhouse and two small villages. It makes sense, considering that the park is along the Agua Fria River. It's also likely that the waters of Lake Pleasant buried additional sites.

You won't have to worry about that at Roadrunner Campground. The developed campground has 72 sites for RV or tent camping, all of which feature water, a dump station, an RV hookup, a ramada, a picnic table, a grill and a fire ring.

Of course, there are great views of the lake from the campground, but you can also take advantage of boating and fishing opportunities, as well as the park's hiking trails, which range from 0.5 to 2 miles in length. Educational programs, guided hikes and stargazing sessions are available through the park's visitors center. In a nutshell, it's easy to create your own history here.

ELEVATION: 1,665 feet

DIRECTIONS: From Interstate 17, north of Phoenix, travel west on State Route 74 (the Carefree Highway) for about 15 miles to Castle Hot Spring Road and turn right. Follow Castle Hot Spring Road to the park entrance.

INFORMATION: Maricopa County Parks & Recreation Department, 602-506-2930 or www.maricopa.gov/parks

SEASON: Year-round

FEE: $25 per night, plus a $6 park entrance fee

RESERVATIONS: No

AMENITIES:

CAMPFIRE TALE: Greater roadrunners are found throughout the Southwest and are known for their long legs and speediness. The birds are known to race down roads in front of vehicles, then dart into roadside brush for safety.

44 | Rock Crossing Campground
Coconino National Forest, Pine

Reconstructed using smashed cars and other recyclable material, the Mogollon Rim's Rock Crossing Campground features spacious sites under canopies of pine trees. Although there are no utility hookups, it is a popular destination for RVs and larger campers, so be prepared for traffic jams along the one-way road that winds around the campground.

Sites 20 and 21 have amazing views of the Rim, and site 24 is no slouch, either. Sites 33 and 35 are good for tents, and all sites feature tables, grills and fire pits, as well as delineated pads on which to pitch your tent. Blue Ridge Reservoir is just 2 miles down the road. Although it more closely resembles a river than a lake, it's a popular spot for fishing and casual kayaking and canoeing. The Arizona Game and Fish Department stocks rainbow trout in the reservoir, so if you're an angler, it should definitely be on your list of destinations.

There's also plenty of wildlife watching. The campground has so many squirrels, you might think the human population is being overrun. They won't bother you, though. They're far too interested in running up and down the pines.

ELEVATION: 7,500 feet

DIRECTIONS: From Pine, travel 26.5 miles north on State Route 87 to Forest Road 751 and turn right. Continue on FR 751 for 2.5 miles to the campground.

INFORMATION: Mogollon Rim Ranger District, Coconino National Forest, 928-477-2255 or www.fs.usda.gov/coconino

SEASON: May through September

FEE: $8 per night (single site); $16 per night (double site)

RESERVATIONS: No

AMENITIES:

CAMPFIRE TALE: Much of the Mogollon Rim is limestone and sandstone. The uppermost segment of the Rim is Coconino sandstone, which spreads all the way across the Colorado Plateau.

5 Sharp Creek Campground
Tonto National Forest, Payson

A paved road winds through this campground, which is separated into group and family areas. Bear right for the family areas. Though sites are close to each other and some are right along the main road, you'll enjoy plenty of open space at Sharp Creek Campground.

Parking places are spacious, and so are tent slabs. Plus, there's room for trailers. The campground is within 10 minutes of Woods Canyon Lake, making it a great starting point for adventures in the woods. The 260 Trailhead is just 3 miles east of the campground, providing access to the Highline National Recreational Trail.

ELEVATION: 6,000 feet

DIRECTIONS: From Payson, travel east on State Route 260 for about 23 miles to the turnoff for the campground, on the right side of the road.

INFORMATION: Payson Ranger District, 928-474-7900 or www.fs.usda.gov/tonto

SEASON: Mid-April through October

FEE: $20 per night

RESERVATIONS: Yes

AMENITIES:

CAMPFIRE TALE: The Highline National Recreational Trail was established in the late 1800s to link homesteads and ranches under the Mogollon Rim. Several trailheads and spurs provide access to the trail, which traverses 51 miles.

6 Spillway Campground
Apache-Sitgreaves National Forests, Payson

Remember the really popular girl from high school? You know the one — she sat behind you in math class. Her hair and nails were perfect, all the boys loved her, and she never had to buy her own ticket to the football game. Consider Spillway Campground that girl.

Adjacent to Woods Canyon Lake, Spillway is the crème de la crème of Mogollon Rim campgrounds. That's mostly because it's just so ... pretty,

coiffed with ponderosa pines, firs and oaks and accessorized with great views of the lake. The 5-mile Woods Canyon Lake Loop Trail begins at the campground and runs around the lake, where you'll find anglers and boaters rejoicing in the scenery. The campground features a paved road, grills and picnic tables, and 26 spacious sites.

Like the girl from math class and because of its charms, Spillway is popular, especially among families. You'll need to get there early to snag a site, especially on weekends. Or set a date — reservations are available here.

ELEVATION: 7,500 feet

DIRECTIONS: From Payson, travel east on State Route 260 for about 30 miles to Forest Road 300 and turn left. Follow FR 300 for about 5 miles to the campground.

INFORMATION: Black Mesa Ranger District, Apache-Sitgreaves National Forests, 928-535-7300 or www.fs.usda.gov/asnf

SEASON: Mid-May through September

FEE: $20 per night

RESERVATIONS: Yes

AMENITIES:

CAMPFIRE TALE: Woods Canyon Lake was formed by an earthen dam along Chevelon Creek. The lake has an average depth of 25 feet and a surface area of 55 acres.

47 | Tortilla Campground
Tonto National Forest, Apache Junction

Just across from Tortilla Flat — the famous tourist destination known for its bikers, burgers and pies — lies Tortilla Campground. This RV- and tent-friendly campground has 70-plus sites that offer sweeping views of lichen-covered canyon walls and the saguaro-speckled boulders of the Superstition Wilderness Area.

Although the campground has amenities, its real charm lies in its proximity to Canyon Lake. There, water recreation abounds, from fishing and boating to just plain lounging. Of course, you're also within a short drive of some of the wilderness area's famous hiking trails, including both First Water and Second Water.

When you return to the campground after a day of adventure, you'll appreciate the spacious campsites, which are equipped with the standard fire pits and grills. If you're just too exhausted to cook, though, there's always a burger just across the road.

Spillway Campground is one of the most popular along the Mogollon Rim. It features 26 sites. ◘ NICK BEREZENKO

ELEVATION: 1,800 feet

DIRECTIONS: From the intersection of Brown Road and the Apache Trail in Apache Junction, travel north on State Route 88 (the Apache Trail) for about 14.5 miles to the campground, which will be on your left. The campground is about 2 miles beyond Canyon Lake.

INFORMATION: Mesa Ranger District, Tonto National Forest, 480-610-3300 or www.fs.usda.gov/tonto

SEASON: Mid-October through April

FEE: A $6 per night Tonto Pass is required.

RESERVATIONS: Yes

AMENITIES: 🚻 🐾 🗑 🚐

CAMPFIRE TALE: During the early 1900s, Tortilla Flat was a popular stop for freight haulers on their way to build Roosevelt Dam. Later, it became a stage stop for tourists on their way to the dam, and it remains a popular tourist attraction today.

48 | White Spar Campground
Prescott National Forest, Prescott

Trees. If you like them, plan a visit to this campground. There are so many here that you won't see much else. But you won't regret choosing from the 56 sites here.

While White Spar's amenities don't differ from those at other campgrounds in this region — picnic tables, fire pits and grills — one feature does stand out: big parking places. That matters, especially if you're traveling with a brood and a lot of gear.

You might use some of that gear to hike or motor along one of the two trails that originate near the campground. The first, the 4.6-mile (one way) Goldwater Lakes Trail 396, is open to hikers and mountain bikers, while the second, School House Gulch Trail 67, is open to motorized vehicles.

After an adventurous day, you won't mind returning to White Spar for a little R&R, and you can thank the trees for a beautiful backdrop.

ELEVATION: 5,700 feet

DIRECTIONS: From Prescott, travel south on Montezuma Street for 3 miles to Forest Road 62 and turn left. The campground will be on your left, just past the Goldwater Lakes Trailhead.

INFORMATION: Bradshaw Ranger District, Prescott National Forest, 928-443-8000 or www.fs.usda.gov/prescott

SEASON: May through October

Canyon Lake is within minutes of Tortilla Campground, along the Apache Trail. 📷 GEORGE STOCKING

FEE: $14 per night

RESERVATIONS: No

AMENITIES: 🚻 🐕 🗑️

CAMPFIRE TALE: More than 800 of Prescott's buildings are listed on the National Register of Historic Buildings, including the 500-seat Elks Opera House.

9 Yavapai Campground
Prescott National Forest, Prescott

If you had to choose one campground to visit in Prescott National Forest, this might be it. With sweeping views of the Granite Dells, a landscape peppered with juniper and manzanita, and its proximity to Granite Basin Lake, Yavapai Campground is a gem.

Its 21 sites include tables, fire pits and grills, and there's plenty of parking. While Yavapai is a great place to stare at the stars and rest your head, you won't want to spend all your time during the day there. That's because you're just 2 miles from Granite Basin Lake, where cattails, blue water and big sky make for some serious photo opportunities.

Of course, water recreation abounds, as well, including fishing, boating, kayaking and canoeing. You might feel as though you've died and stepped into a Bob Ross painting — the lake is that beautiful. Plus, you can picnic under happy little trees.

ELEVATION: 5,600 feet

DIRECTIONS: From the corner of Iron Springs and Williamson Valley roads in Prescott, take Iron Springs Road for about 3 miles to Granite Basin Road. Turn right and continue on Granite Basin Road for approximately 2.1 miles to the campground, which will be on your left.

INFORMATION: Bradshaw Ranger District, Prescott National Forest, 928-443-8000 or www.fs.usda.gov/prescott

SEASON: May through October

FEE: $18 per night

RESERVATIONS: No

AMENITIES: 🚻 🐕 🗑️

CAMPFIRE TALE: The Granite Dells are made of bedrock and granite and have an appearance that might best be described as lumpy. Geologists have dated the granite at 1.4 billion years old and have noted an unusually high uranium content in the rocks.

The Granite Dells and Watson Lake are popular among rock climbers and water recreationists and are within minutes of Yavapai Campground. 📷 JEFF KIDA

Luna Lake
📷 PAUL GILL

EASTERN ARIZONA CAMPGROUNDS

From alpine-flanked meadows to ponderosa-lined streams, when it comes to camping in Eastern Arizona, the White Mountains should be at the top of your list. Although the Wallow Fire of 2011 burned parts of the Apache-Sitgreaves National Forests, recreation areas are open for business and just as gorgeous as before. That's not to say that the area near Safford, in the southeastern section of the state, isn't equally stunning. The Pinaleño Mountains and the campgrounds therein offer amazing high-elevation camping — perfect for summer. Whether your Eastern Arizona adventures take you north or south, you'll find beautiful campgrounds and scenery.

Alpine Divide Campground
Apache-Sitgreaves National Forests, Alpine

Quaint. That might be the first word that comes to mind when you pitch your tent at Alpine Divide Campground. Rustic. Primitive. Charming. Those work, too. No matter what word you choose, at Alpine Divide, you'll get a real sense of forest camping, thanks to the ponderosa pines and bracken ferns.

Just off U.S. Route 191 north of Alpine, the campground has only 12 sites. There are no utility hookups, but each site includes a picnic table, a fire ring and a grill. Vault toilets and potable water round out the amenities, but chances are that if you're camping here, you're not too concerned with whether you can shower, shave and fluff your hair in the morning. Though much of Escudilla Mountain and its trails were badly damaged during the Wallow Fire, some of the trails have reopened. If you hike them, you're likely to see young aspens. For wildlife- and bird-watching, Hulsey and Lyman lakes are nearby, as is Sunrise Park Resort, a skiing and snowboarding destination that also has summer recreation.

So while Alpine Divide is a quaint little campground, this is big country with plenty of opportunities for adventure.

ELEVATION: 8,840 feet

DIRECTIONS: From Alpine, travel north on U.S. Route 191 for about 4 miles to the campground.

VEHICLE REQUIREMENTS: None

INFORMATION: Springerville Ranger District, Apache-Sitgreaves National Forests, 928-333-4301 or www.fs.usda.gov/asnf

SEASON: Mid-May through mid-September

FEE: $10 per night

RESERVATIONS: Yes

AMENITIES:

CAMPFIRE TALE: Named for the Spanish word for "bowl," Escudilla Mountain tops out at 10,912 feet, which makes it a toddler compared with the 12,637-foot Humphreys Peak in Flagstaff.

Apache Trout Campground
Apache-Sitgreaves National Forests, Springerville

Big Lake is, in fact, big. The 575-acre Big Lake Recreation Area plays host to outdoor activities such as hiking, mountain biking, wildlife watching and trout fishing. It also welcomes nature-loving campers with open arms.

Four campgrounds are within the recreation area, the gem of which is Apache Trout. Circled with paved roads and chock-full of amenities, this campground is an ideal destination for families and first-time campers.

It's one of the bigger campgrounds in the area, so while you're enjoying Mother Nature, don't be surprised if you run into large numbers of your outdoorsy brethren. Tents, trailers and motorhomes are welcome at this hosted campground, which features 44 full-hookup sites, flush toilets, showers, drinking water, firewood, fire rings, picnic tables, a dump station and a boat launch. A marina doubles as a full-service store.

Because White Mountains campgrounds like this one are popular in summer, visitors should be prepared for heavy rains that can roll in with the monsoons, particularly in July and August. Also be aware of deer, skunks and bears, which are common campground visitors. Steer clear and don't feed the animals. While Big Lake may be big, it's a small world from a shared-space perspective. Respect the animals, and they'll respect you.

ELEVATION: 9,100 feet

DIRECTIONS: From Springerville, travel south on State Route 261 for about 25 miles to Big Lake Recreation Area.

INFORMATION: Springerville Ranger District, Apache-Sitgreaves National Forests, 928-333-4301 or www.fs.usda.gov/asnf

SEASON: Mid-May through mid-September

FEE: $24 per night

RESERVATIONS: Yes

AMENITIES:

CAMPFIRE TALE: The Apache trout, or Arizona trout, is the state fish of Arizona. In fact, *Oncorhynchus gilae apache* is one of only two species of trout native to the Grand Canyon State. The other is *Oncorhynchus gilae,* or the Gila trout.

52 | Benny Creek Campground
Apache-Sitgreaves National Forests, Greer

The road to Benny Creek Campground meanders through a stand of ponderosa pines before snuggling up between meadows to one side and views of Bunch Reservoir on the other. It's a pretty precursor to this lush, tree-covered White Mountains campground, which overlooks its name-sake creek.

There are 26 spacious sites, all with soft dirt. That doesn't sound like an amenity, but think about it — if you're going to pitch a tent and sleep on the ground, wouldn't you rather it be on a soft surface instead of a rocky, ragged one? There's nothing ragged, rocky or rickety about this hosted campground, which features picnic tables, fire rings and grills at

Benny Creek Campground is in a pine forest that overlooks Benny Creek. 📷 PAUL GILL

every site. Although there are no utility hookups, the sites accommodate trailers and motorhomes up to 24 feet in length.

No matter how you cruise into Benny Creek, be on the lookout for creatures great and small. Deer, chipmunks and Abert's squirrels are known to frequent the campground.

ELEVATION: 8,250 feet

DIRECTIONS: From Greer, travel 2.5 miles north on State Route 373 to the campground, which will be on your right.

INFORMATION: Springerville Ranger District, Apache-Sitgreaves National Forests, 928-333-4301 or www.fs.usda.gov/asnf

SEASON: May through September

FEE: $10 per night

RESERVATIONS: Yes

AMENITIES:

CAMPFIRE TALE: Abert's squirrels are named for Colonel John James Abert, a naturalist who headed the Corps of Topographical Engineers.

53 | Black Canyon Rim Campground
Apache-Sitgreaves National Forests, Heber

Although it's possible to camp along Forest Road 300, the heavily traveled Mogollon Rim route that accesses this campground, doing so would be devoid of the amenities found at Black Canyon Rim Campground. This private destination has 21 large sites tucked beneath ponderosa pines. Because sites are so spacious, you won't feel as though you're right on top of your neighbor. It also helps that this destination isn't the most popular in the White Mountains, especially among families, who seem to prefer camping at Fool Hollow Lake and other more developed sites that are a bit closer to larger towns.

That's not to say Black Canyon Rim isn't family-friendly. Just minutes from Black Canyon Lake, this is a great spot for campers who like to take to the water for a little relaxation. Fishing and boating are popular, but if you're into more terrestrial relaxation, wildlife-watching opportunities are many. Deer, squirrels, chipmunks and the occasional elk frequent the area, as do several bird species. Or, if you're of the I'd-like-a-little-history-with-my-getaway persuasion, cruise FR 300. You'll find the marker that commemorates the Battle of Big Dry Wash, which took place along the Mogollon Rim in 1882. It was the last Apache-versus-Army battle in Arizona.

ELEVATION: 7,600 feet

DIRECTIONS: From Heber, travel 18 miles west on State Route 260 to Forest Road 300 and turn left, following the signs to Black Canyon Lake. Continue on FR 300 for 2.5 miles to Forest Road 86 and turn left. The campground will be on your right.

INFORMATION: Springerville Ranger District, Apache-Sitgreaves National Forests, 928-333-4301 or www.fs.usda.gov/asnf

SEASON: May through November

FEE: $14 per night

RESERVATIONS: Yes

AMENITIES:

CAMPFIRE TALE: The Battle of Big Dry Wash is believed to have been sparked, in part, by the cavalry's 1881 attack on an Apache ghost dance along Cibecue Creek. During that attack, cavalry soldiers killed Apache prophet Nock-ay-det-klinne.

54 | Buffalo Crossing Campground
Apache-Sitgreaves National Forests, Alpine

There's something romantic about this campground. Maybe it's the meadows. Maybe it's the ample picnic areas. Maybe it's the song of the Black River. No matter what it is, it's beautiful, and it makes this a great place to pitch your tent for a few days.

Situated along the east fork of the Black River, Buffalo Crossing is accessed via Forest Road 24A, a pretty side road flanked by quaking aspens, including many young ones that emerged after the Wallow Fire. Sixteen large sites back up to either a big, boulder-strewn hillside or the grassy banks of the river, and among the amenities are picnic tables, grills and fire pits. Site 11 is nestled in a grove of yellow-bellies, as are sites 14, 15 and 16. Although those might be the shadiest, prettiest spots, there really are no duds at Buffalo Crossing, which was named for the behemoth bovines that once roamed the state.

It's unlikely you'll encounter a moseying buffalo near the campground these days, but if you cast a line into the Black River, you may come up with one of several species of trout, including rainbow, brook, brown and Apache. So if you feel the urge to be active during your stay at Buffalo Crossing, fishing is a good bet. Otherwise, just mosey.

ELEVATION: 7,540 feet

DIRECTIONS: From Alpine, travel 2 miles north on U.S. Route 191 to Forest Road 249. Travel west on FR 249 for about 5 miles and turn left on Forest Road 276. Follow FR 276 to its junction with Forest Roads 24 and 25. Turn left onto FR 24, where you'll see signs for the campground, then continue on FR24A for 0.5 miles to Buffalo Crossing.

INFORMATION: Springerville Ranger District, Apache-Sitgreaves National Forests, 928-333-4301 or www.fs.usda.gov/asnf

SEASON: May through October

FEE: $10 per night

RESERVATIONS: No

AMENITIES: 🚻 🐕 📷 🗑

CAMPFIRE TALE: In Arizona, buffalo are found in two wildlife management areas operated by the Arizona Game and Fish Department — Raymond, east of Flagstaff, and House Rock, east of North Kaibab.

55 | Cunningham Campground
Coronado National Forest, Safford

Tucked between Grant and Moonshine creeks near the top of Mount Graham, this fairly primitive campground was spruced up as part of the American Reinvestment and Recovery Act of 2009. Shaded by elegant stands of aspens and firs, Cunningham is the starting point for several hiking trails, including the Grant Creek and Grant Goudy Ridge trails, both of which reference Fort Grant, the former Army post on the southwestern slope of the mountain.

But easy access to Pinaleño Mountains hiking trails isn't the only thing that makes this campground special. It also features a corral, uncommon at campgrounds in the state. So, if you're a traveler by horseback, this is a great place to tether your mount for the night. Car campers won't be disappointed, either. Ten sites feature fire pits and grills, and aspens surround most of them, particularly 2 and 9.

The only downside to camping here during the warm summer months? Bugs. Lots of them. Although they're easily dissuaded by sprays and screens, they can be annoying while you're searching for repellent in your backpack. If you can handle the bold bugs, you won't regret parking your steed — steel or saddled — at Cunningham.

ELEVATION: 9,000 feet

DIRECTIONS: From Safford, travel south on U.S. Route 191 for 8 miles to State Route 366 and turn right. Follow SR 366 for 26 miles to the campground.

INFORMATION: Safford Ranger District, Coronado National Forest, 928-428-4150 or www.fs.usda.gov/coronado

SEASON: Mid-April through mid-November

FEE: $10 per night

RESERVATIONS: No

AMENITIES: 🚻 🐕

CAMPFIRE TALE: The Army abandoned Fort Grant in 1905, but after Arizona gained statehood in 1912, it became the Fort Grant

---

The meadow at Cunningham Campground, in the Pinaleño Mountains, blooms with black-eyed Susans and bracken ferns during the summer. 📷 RANDY PRENTICE

Fool Hollow Lake and its campground are popular among families. The lake is in Show Low. 📷 MOREY K. MILBRADT

State Industrial School. Decades later, in 1968, the state assigned Fort Grant to the Department of Corrections. Today, it's a unit of the Arizona State Prison Complex at Safford.

56 | Diamond Rock Campground
Apache-Sitgreaves National Forests, Alpine

The Black River doesn't hold a candle to the Colorado. How could it, really? It's shorter — its main stem runs only 45 miles — and it's not nearly as wide. But this little river is magical in its own right. You'll experience its charms at Diamond Rock Campground, a stunning site on the river's east fork. To get there, you'll use the same roads, Forest Roads 249 and 276, that you would to access Big Lake Recreation Area.

Meadows, pines, aspens — the road meanders through them all, popping in and out of forest groves, through cow pastures and along granite cliffs — then, as you turn onto Forest Road 276, you may think for a moment or two that you're in Ireland or Scotland. The scenery is green, green, green and the open space is big, big, big. After about 6 miles, you'll approach the campground, which features 12 single sites with fire rings and grills. Three of them — sites 7, 11 and 12 — have three-sided,

Adirondack-style shelters that were built by the Civilian Conservation Corps. They're perfect rainy-weather amenities, but here's hoping that you experience nothing but sunny skies during your stay at Diamond Rock — sunny skies and the pretty Black River, just steps from the campground.

ELEVATION: 7,890 feet

DIRECTIONS: From Alpine, travel north on U.S. Route 191 for about 2 miles to Forest Road 249 (the turnoff to Big Lake). Follow FR 249 for 5.2 miles to where the road forks. Bear left onto Forest Road 276. Follow FR 276 for about 6 miles to the campground.

INFORMATION: Springerville Ranger District, Apache-Sitgreaves National Forests, 928-333-4301 or www.fs.usda.gov/asnf

SEASON: May through October

FEE: $10 per night

RESERVATIONS: Yes

AMENITIES:

CAMPFIRE TALE: From 1933 to 1942, about 53,000 men worked on Civilian Conservation Corps projects in Arizona. They received roughly $30 in pay each month.

7 | Fool Hollow Lake Campground
Fool Hollow Lake State Park, Show Low

In 1885, Thomas Jefferson Adair moved to the Show Low area. He was dead set on farming, an idea so absurd to the locals that they declared "only a fool would try to farm the place." As it turns out, the locals were right. Now, a lake covers the town that was once named for the hapless farmer. The 150-acre man-made pool is just part of the 800-acre Fool Hollow Lake Recreation Area in the Apache-Sitgreaves National Forests near Show Low.

You'll find a developed campground that features 31 tent sites and 92 sites with hookups for RVs, along with some of the finest amenities in the area: showers, flush toilets, an amphitheater, a walking trail and playgrounds. The day-use area has covered picnic spots. If ever there were a family-friendly campground in the White Mountains, this is it.

Of course, there's also Fool Hollow Lake. Sites 23 through 31 have the most stunning views of the lake and the surrounding juniper- and wild-flower-speckled meadows. Fishing, swimming and boating are allowed. The lake is known to host great blue herons in addition to happy camp-ers, so keep your eyes peeled for a view of the majestic birds.

ELEVATION: 6,300 feet

DIRECTIONS: From Show Low, travel west on Deuce of Clubs to Old Linden Road and turn right. The campground is at 1500 N. Fool Hollow Lake Road.

INFORMATION: Arizona State Parks, Fool Hollow Lake Recreation Area,

928-537-3680 or www.azstateparks.com/parks/foho

SEASON: Year-round

FEE: $17 per night (non-electric site); $30 per night (electric site)

RESERVATIONS: Yes, 520-586-2283

AMENITIES:

CAMPFIRE TALE: **Show Low was named when settlers C.E. Cooley and Marion Clark decided the town just wasn't big enough for the both of them. So, they played a hand of cards. "If you can show low, you win," Clark said. Cooley turned the deuce of clubs. And so Show Low was.**

58 | Hannagan Meadow Campground
Apache-Sitgreaves National Forests, Hannagan Meadow

There's something magical about Hannagan Meadow. Maybe it's the morning dew and the not-so-distant bugling of elk. Maybe it's because the cellphone that gets reception here is a rare, special cellphone. Maybe it's just because Hannagan Meadow is, hands down, the crown jewel of the Apache-Sitgreaves National Forests.

The campground isn't chock-full of amenities like some of the others in the region, but it is one of the most popular. That's likely because of its scenery — stately ponderosas, mostly — and wildlife. Birds and squirrels chatter away in the trees, and elk are common. For amenities, you'll find spacious sites and potable water, and for a song — Hannagan Meadow is a no-fee campground.

When you're not watching for wildlife near your tent, it is possible to venture out on Aker Lake Trail, which originates at the campground between sites 6 and 7. The moderately rated trail is 3.5 miles one way, and leads to its namesake body of water via a mixed forest of aspens and conifers as well as the Butterfly Cienega meadow. Along the way will be even more birds and the occasional mule deer or even a black bear. Have your camera handy and watch from a distance. You might capture a frame-worthy photograph and a magical memory all your own. Although the trail experienced significant damage during the Wallow Fire of 2011, grasses and young trees are emerging from the ash and, at press time, cleanup was under way to restore trail clarity.

ELEVATION: 9,120 feet

DIRECTIONS: From Alpine, travel south on U.S. Route 191 for about 22 miles to Hannagan Meadow. The campground is 0.25 miles south of Hannagan

Stars blanket Hannagan Meadow, a must-visit destination in Arizona's White Mountains. JEFF KIDA

Meadow Lodge on the west side of U.S. 191.

INFORMATION: Alpine Ranger District, Apache-Sitgreaves National Forests, 928-339-5000 or www.fs.usda.gov/asnf

SEASON: May through September

FEE: None

RESERVATIONS: None

AMENITIES: 🚻 🏠 🚰

CAMPFIRE TALE: During summer, elk range within a half-mile of water, which means they're common in higher elevations. There they will stay until snow forces them to lower elevations and easier access to food — weeds, grasses and shrubs.

59 Hospital Flat Campground
Coronado National Forest, Safford

Situated along Grant Creek on the southern slope of the Pinaleño Mountains, Hospital Flat Campground is named for the 1880s field hospital that once existed there. Although the hospital, which served soldiers from nearby Fort Grant, closed in 1905, the sunny meadow where it stood remains.

The campground features a 0.75-mile self-guided nature trail, as well as that pretty meadow and its wildflowers. Wild onions, rhubarb and ponderosas also grow there. It seems, too, that flies are drawn to the meadow as much as campers are. That's a common trait of these Swift Trail campgrounds, but not something that should deter you from a visit.

Besides, you'll be too focused on the scenery to let the bugs bother you. Several campgrounds run up Mount Graham, but Hospital Flat is one of the prettiest. It's also near several hiking trails, including the Grant Hill and Cunningham Loop trails. History, hiking and hillside views. You can't ask much more from a campground, and Hospital Flat delivers.

ELEVATION: 9,000 feet

DIRECTIONS: From Safford, travel south on U.S. Route 191 for 8 miles to State Route 366 and turn right. Follow SR 366 for 23 miles to the campground.

INFORMATION: Safford Ranger District, Coronado National Forest, 928-428-4150 or www.fs.usda.gov/coronado

SEASON: Mid-April through mid-November

FEE: $10 per night

RESERVATIONS: No

AMENITIES: 🚻 🏠 🚰

CAMPFIRE TALE: The Mount Graham red squirrel is native to the Pinaleño Mountains. The endangered subspecies of the American red squirrel is smaller than most subspecies and lacks the white-tipped black tail common to red squirrels.

0 KP Cienega Campground
Apache-Sitgreaves National Forests, Hannagan Meadow

If you're afraid of heights, don't camp here. It's that simple. Even though it's not on the edge of anything, at about 9,000 feet, KP Cienega Campground is one of the highest in Arizona. It's also secluded, and more popular among deer, elk, black bears and squirrels than it is among people.

Campers access the campground via Forest Road 55. About a mile in, you'll notice a beautiful meadow to your right. Don't be surprised to see Steller's jays or rare Northern goshawks flitting about. Not even a half-mile farther down the road, you'll come to KP Trail 70, a strenuous, 9-mile hike that wanders along the south fork of KP Creek as it ambles toward the Blue River. You'll also see a burn area that predates the 2011 Wallow Fire — it's experiencing a rebirth of vegetation.

The campground and its five sites lie just beyond the burn area. Although KP Cienega is small, it's mighty in beauty — grasses, ferns, enormous pines, and Colorado blue and Engelmann spruces. This is Arizona's backcountry at its finest.

ELEVATION: 9,000 feet

DIRECTIONS: From Hannagan Meadow, travel 4.75 miles south on U.S. Route 191 to Forest Road 55 and turn left. The campground is 1.3 miles down FR 55.

INFORMATION: Alpine Ranger District, Apache-Sitgreaves National Forests, 928-339-5000 or www.fs.usda.gov/asnf

SEASON: April through September

FEE: None

RESERVATIONS: No

AMENITIES:

CAMPFIRE TALE: *Cienega* is a Spanish Colonial term for a spring. It's used in the Southwest to describe a marshy or grassy area in a canyon or at the foot of a mountain.

51 Lakeside Campground
Apache-Sitgreaves National Forests, Lakeside

This is a spot for campers looking for a quick getaway. Situated within Lakeside town limits, the 82-unit campground is RV-friendly and popular among families. Because of its urban location, it's also crowded, so reservations are accepted.

The campground is similar in many ways to Fort Tuthill County Park Campground in Flagstaff (see page 36) in that sites are close to each other, creating a fun, communal experience. Ponderosa pines make for a forest feel despite the municipal setting.

Although sites are equipped with the standard fire pits and grills, you may grow tired of camp fare. Luckily, the campground is adjacent to Mama Bear's restaurant.

ELEVATION: 6,950 feet

DIRECTIONS: Lakeside Campground is on State Route 260 in Lakeside, across the highway from Lakeside Ranger Station.

INFORMATION: Lakeside Ranger District, Apache-Sitgreaves National Forests, 928-368-2100 or www.fs.usda.gov/asnf

SEASON: May through September

FEE: $12 per night

RESERVATIONS: Yes

AMENITIES:

CAMPFIRE TALE: Founded by Mormon pioneers in the early 1880s, Lakeside derived its name from the area's lakes.

2 | Los Burros Campground
Apache-Sitgreaves National Forests, McNary

If you're looking for a getaway off the beaten path, this is it. From McNary, Los Burros Campground is accessed via a gravel road that runs through the San Carlos Apache Reservation. The road is easy to miss, so look for signs that indicate Cady/Apache County Road 3140 and Vernon. Once you've made the turn from McNary, the journey to the campground is simple — and downright pretty, especially if you like pine trees, ferns and a scattering of wildflowers and grasses.

After about 3.5 miles, you'll come to a stand of aspens on each side of the road, evidence that you've climbed in elevation. But almost as quickly as you enter the stand, you're out of it again. At the 5-mile mark, you'll enter the Sitgreaves National Forest, and at 7 miles, you'll reach the campground.

This no-fee area is characterized by beautiful meadows and the remnants of a ranger station that was built between 1909 and 1910. The fireguard who lived there rode his horse to the fire lookout each day and gathered water from Los Burros Spring, which is just east of the big red barn. Enormous ponderosa pines and aspens surround it and everything

Campsites at Los Burros, north of McNary, are situated in meadows and wooded areas. 📷 PAUL GILL else at the 10-site campground. While Los Burros is out of the way, it's worth every extra mile.

ELEVATION: 7,900 feet

DIRECTIONS: From McNary, take Vernon/Cady Road (County Road 3140) north for 7 miles to the campground.

INFORMATION: Springerville Ranger District, Apache-Sitgreaves National Forests, 928-333-4301 or www.fs.usda.gov/asnf

SEASON: May through October

FEE: None

RESERVATIONS: No

AMENITIES: 🚻 🏕️

CAMPFIRE TALE: The San Carlos Apache Reservation spans 1.86 million acres and is home to the world's largest deposit of peridot, the green stone also known as "heart of the Earth" and "stone of the sun."

63 Luna Lake Campground
Apache-Sitgreaves National Forests, Alpine

Luna Lake is the largest campground in the Alpine Ranger District. Even during peak season, you're likely to find a site here. Bordering its namesake lake, the campground is well developed and features a boat ramp, a tackle shop and plenty of motorhome and trailer parking.

Water recreation rules at Luna Lake, and fishing is particularly popular, thanks to regularly stocked rainbow trout. Wildflower meadows that surround a grove of ponderosa pines will appeal to campers who prefer to explore on foot, and wildlife-viewing opportunities, including elk and wild turkeys, abound.

Mountain biking and hiking trails criss-cross the area near the lake, and Blue River Road begins just across from the campground. The scenic route meanders into the heart of Blue Range Primitive Area. Back at Luna Lake, try to snag site 25 or 27 — they have the best views.

ELEVATION: 7,960 feet

DIRECTIONS: From Alpine, travel east on U.S. Route 180 for 3.8 miles to Luna Lake Recreation Area. Follow the gravel road (Forest Road 570) for 1.5 miles to the campground.

INFORMATION: Alpine Ranger District, Apache-Sitgreaves National Forests, 928-339-5000 or www.fs.usda.gov/asnf

SEASON: April through September

FEE: $12 per night

RESERVATIONS: Yes

AMENITIES: 🚻 🏕️ 🗑️

CAMPFIRE TALE: Luna Lake Wildlife Area provides a riparian habitat for birds, mammals, fish and amphibians, including bats, bald eagles, tree frogs, weasels and elk.

4 Raccoon Campground
Apache-Sitgreaves National Forests, Alpine

Raccoons aren't exactly fickle creatures. They'll eat pretty much anything — garbage, fish, mice, eggs, insects. They're also fond of forests, which is why you're likely to spot a few at this aptly named campground.

Situated along the east fork of the Black River, this campground is characterized by lush greenery and granite-stacked hillsides. Access to the river is easy, although campsites are several feet away from the stream to protect its banks.

Natural beauty is surely the draw here, as the campground is small and rustic. Each of the 10 sites is equipped with the standard fire pits and grills. Ponderosas and alders make it easy to get lost in a Mother Nature-inspired reverie. Should you hear a rustling next to you, though, check to make sure you didn't fall asleep with an open bag of pork rinds nearby. Chances are, one of the campground's namesake critters is paying you a visit.

ELEVATION: 7,600 feet

DIRECTIONS: From Alpine, travel north on U.S. Route 191 for about 2 miles to Forest Road 249 and turn left. Continue on FR 249 for 5 miles to Forest Road 276 and turn left. Continue on FR 276 for 6 miles to East Fork Recreation Area.

INFORMATION: Alpine Ranger District, Apache-Sitgreaves National Forests, 928-339-5000 or www.fs.usda.gov/asnf

SEASON: May through October

FEE: $10 per night

RESERVATIONS: No

AMENITIES:

CAMPFIRE TALE: Raccoons can be found throughout the United States, and although scientists once thought they were solitary animals, they're now known to be social creatures. Related females share common areas, while unrelated males live together in groups of four or six.

5 Riggs Flat Campground
Coronado National Forest, Safford

Riggs Flat Campground may be the finest of campgrounds in the Safford area. Near the top of Mount Graham in the Pinaleño Mountains, the campground is reminiscent of something Rockwellian — think little boys fishing on the banks of Riggs Lake, and dads prepping a barbecued feast.

Indeed, fishing and boating in the bright blue waters of the 11-acre lake are this campground's main draws, as are wildlife viewing and cool mountain air. Soldier Creek Campground is nearby, and there you'll find the Grant Goudy Ridge hiking trail, which heads down Mount Graham to Fort Grant.

Back at Riggs Flat, there are 31 individual campsites and one smallish group-camping site. There are warnings about black bears, so be bear aware and take this advice from the Forest Service: "To avoid putting a bear's life in danger and risking the loss of some of your own property, please dispose of all garbage in the bear-proof containers provided. Also, remember to keep all food out of reach and out of sight of these curious and powerful animals." That means you, dads.

ELEVATION: 8,600 feet

DIRECTIONS: From Safford, travel south on U.S. Route 191 for 8 miles to State Route 366 and turn right. Continue on SR 366 for 29 miles to the Columbine Visitors Information Station, then continue along Forest Roads 803 and 287 for about 5 miles to the campground.

INFORMATION: Safford Ranger District, Coronado National Forest, 928-428-4150 or www.fs.usda.gov/coronado

SEASON: Mid-April through mid-November

FEE: $10 per night

RESERVATIONS: No

AMENITIES: 🚻 🐾

CAMPFIRE TALE: The Arizona Game and Fish Department financed the dam that formed Riggs Flat Lake in 1957. Today, the department stocks it with brown, brook and rainbow trout.

66 | Rolfe C. Hoyer Campground
Apache-Sitgreaves National Forests, Greer

This well-developed campground is just down the road from Benny Creek. With 91 sites, Rolfe C. Hoyer is one of the largest campgrounds in the area, and thanks to spacious sites, an amphitheater, showers, an educational program and "delicious and drinkable" well water (per the camp host), it's also one of the most popular among families.

While the amenities garner an A-plus, so, too, does the scenery. As at

---

Riggs Flat Campground is located at its namesake lake, at the top of Mount Graham, near Safford. 📷 RANDY PRENTICE

so many campgrounds in the area, ponderosa pines take center stage, but Rolfe C. Hoyer is also just across the road from the beautiful Greer Lakes, where fishing and boating opportunities abound. Be prepared, though. During July and August, heavy rain is common, and because of the campground's elevation — about 8,000 feet — evenings can be downright chilly.

If you forget a sweatshirt, the tiny White Mountains hamlet of Greer is 2 miles south and a great place to get gas and stock up on groceries. That is, of course, if you're willing to leave Rolfe C. Hoyer.

ELEVATION: 8,300 feet

DIRECTIONS: From Greer, travel north on State Route 373 for about 2 miles to the campground, which will be on your left.

INFORMATION: Springerville Ranger District, Apache-Sitgreaves National Forests, 928-333-4301 or www.fs.usda.gov/asnf

SEASON: Mid-May through September

FEE: $16 per night

RESERVATIONS: Yes

AMENITIES:

CAMPFIRE TALE: The Greer Lakes comprise three individual lakes — Bunch, River and Tunnel. River Reservoir is known for its population of brown trout and once boasted the largest brown trout caught in Arizona.

67 | Strayhorse Campground
Apache-Sitgreaves National Forests, Hannagan Meadow

As its name implies, Strayhorse Campground is horse-friendly. But, oddly, you won't find many horses here. Nor will you find many people.

Strayhorse is remote and easy to miss, which makes it romantic in a sense. Adding to its appeal is its rain shelter. It's easy to imagine cozying up underneath it and a blanket or two when a summer storm rolls through. No-fee campsites are on both sides of the highway, with four sites on the west side of the road and two on the east side. Each has a picnic table and a fire pit, which will come in handy should you decide to hike the Highline National Recreational Trail, which winds for 51 miles. You'll find the trailhead at Strayhorse.

The trail winds into Chitty Creek, climbing in and out of drainages and following the bottom of the Mogollon Rim. Raspberry Trail 35 also originates from the campground and wanders into Blue Range Primitive Area. Whichever trail you choose, you'll no doubt be hungry when you return to Strayhorse, so make good use of those fire pits. And, bring plenty of your own drinking water. Water spigots at Strayhorse only work seasonally.

ELEVATION: 7,780 feet

DIRECTIONS: From Hannagan Meadow, travel south on U.S. Route 191 for 10.5 miles to the campground.

INFORMATION: Alpine Ranger District, Apache-Sitgreaves National Forests, 928-339-5000 or www.fs.usda.gov/asnf

SEASON: April through November

FEE: None

RESERVATIONS: No

AMENITIES:

CAMPFIRE TALE: **The Blue Range was the last designated primitive area in the United States, having been appointed as such in 1933. It comprises 173,762 acres and is home to the endangered Mexican gray wolf, reintroduced there in 1998 as part of a federal recovery program for the species.**

8 | West Fork Campground
Apache-Sitgreaves National Forests, Alpine

Forest Road 25 is wide, graveled and generally easy to manage. It runs through massive stands of ponderosa pines and across meadows. After you've traveled it for just under a mile, you'll cross the west fork of the Black River, and, after 1.2 miles, you'll encounter a log cabin to your right. It sits in the middle of a wildflower-covered meadow. This is stunning country. So stunning, it could easily serve as the setting for a romantic novel.

Then, you'll come to Forest Road 68 and receive a warning about the narrow, rough road. It's rough, indeed, but not so narrow that you'll be white-knuckling the steering wheel for the entire journey. This is the road you'll follow for about 3 miles to West Fork Campground.

Spacious and spread out, campsites are surrounded by enormous pines. And, of course, the Black River is right here — just don't dig worms along its banks. Signs are posted to that effect, giving fair warning to anglers itching to drop their lines in the river in search of trout.

Should a storm roll in, Adirondack shelters will protect both you and your gear, and when the weather clears, you'll find no shortage of things to do, from mountain-biking to hiking to bird-watching. Just remember to leave the worms for the birds.

ELEVATION: 7,740 feet

DIRECTIONS: From Alpine, travel north on U.S. Route 191 for about 2 miles to Forest Road 249 and turn left. Continue on FR 249 for 5 miles to Forest Road 276 and turn left. Follow FR 276 for about 13 miles to Forest Road 25 (at Buffalo Crossing). Continue on FR 25 for 3 miles to Forest Road 68 and proceed to the campground.

INFORMATION: Alpine Ranger District, Apache-Sitgreaves National Forests, 928-339-5000 or www.fs.usda.gov/asnf

SEASON: May through October

FEE: None

RESERVATIONS: No

AMENITIES: 🚻 🐕

CAMPFIRE TALE: **Rainbow trout, common in the Black River, are cannibals of sorts: They eat the eggs of other fish species. The maximum recorded life span for a rainbow trout is 11 years.**

9 | Winn Campground
Apache-Sitgreaves National Forests, Greer

This campground is big, convenient and a great place for hikers and anglers to spend the night. Why? Because it's right next to the Mount Baldy trailheads and both the east and west forks of the Little Colorado River.

With 63 individual sites on a red dirt road in two separate loops — Bobcat and Deer — the campground is surrounded by hillsides and offers great views of meadows. This is wide-open country, and there's enough big sky to go around. The same goes for the aspens on Bobcat Loop. There are plenty of grassy areas, perfect for tossing a Frisbee or a football or just lounging around, soaking in the scenery.

Although water is available at the entrance to Winn, it's not throughout the rest of the grounds, so pack plenty of your own.

ELEVATION: 9,320 feet

DIRECTIONS: From Greer, travel southwest on State Route 373 and Forest Road 87 for approximately 12 miles to State Route 273 and turn left. Follow SR 273 to Forest Road 54. Turn left and follow FR 54 for 1.2 miles to the campground.

INFORMATION: Springerville Ranger District, Apache-Sitgreaves National Forests, 928-333-4301 or www.fs.usda.gov/asnf

SEASON: Mid-May through October

FEE: $14 per night

RESERVATIONS: Yes

AMENITIES: 🚻 🏠

CAMPFIRE TALE: **West Baldy Trail 94 follows the west fork of the Little Colorado River, climbing until it meets East Baldy Trail beneath Mount Thomas. The summit of Mount Baldy is on the White Mountain Apache Reservation and is open to tribal members only.**

Musk mallow blooms along the west fork of the Black River. 📷 PAUL GILL

The Huachuca Mountains
📷 RANDY PRENTICE

SOUTHERN ARIZONA CAMPGROUNDS

A few of the campgrounds in this chapter are named for historic figures — General Hitchcock and Cochise Stronghold, for example. Others are named for their scenic beauty — Lakeview and Rose Canyon. The names of others will make you furrow your brow and wonder, "How did that name come to be?" No matter which campgrounds you choose to visit in Southern Arizona, you won't be disappointed. Whether camping in the Dragoons, retracing Geronimo's footsteps in the Chiricahuas or soaking up the cool forest setting of Madera Canyon, you're bound to find adventure.

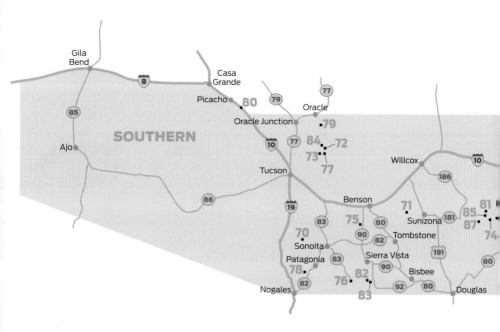

0 | Bog Springs Campground
Coronado National Forest, Tucson

Tucked away inside Madera Canyon, Bog Springs Campground is paradise found. Agaves, junipers and big boulders decorate this small oasis, and an intricate network of hiking and biking trails begins here. Deer dart in and out of the surrounding forest, and you might even spot a turkey or four crossing the road — a group of Abbey Road-inspired gobblers.

Turkeys aren't the only birds you'll see in Madera Canyon. Known worldwide for its migratory bird species, the canyon is home to the elusive elegant trogon. With red bellies and metallic green heads, the males are a sight to see. Pack your camera just in case.

Campground amenities include sites with stone foundations and the standard picnic tables, fire pits and grills. Johns are just across from the Dutch John Spring trailhead. Insert your own joke here. While the amenities are nice, the scenery is the real draw of Bog Springs Campground — just ask the deer, turkeys and trogons.

ELEVATION: 5,060 feet

DIRECTIONS: From Tucson, travel south on Interstate 19 for 24 miles to the Continental Road exit and turn left. Follow Continental Road and signs for Madera Canyon for 13 miles to the campground.

INFORMATION: Santa Catalina Ranger District, Coronado National Forest, 520-749-8700 or www.fs.usda.gov/coronado

SEASON: Year-round

FEE: $10 per night

RESERVATIONS: No

AMENITIES:

CAMPFIRE TALE: One of the most popular bicycle trails in the Madera Canyon area is Elephant Head Trail. It originates from Madera Canyon Recreation Area and ends at the Fred Lawrence Whipple Observatory's visitors center, some 13 miles away.

71 | Cochise Stronghold Campground
Coronado National Forest, Pearce

Legends were born in the Dragoon Mountains. There, Chiricahua Apache leader Cochise hid from and battled his enemies, and there he's buried. "I have drunk the waters of the Dragoon Mountains, and they have cooled me," Cochise is believed to have said. "I do not want to leave here."

After a visit to Cochise Stronghold Campground, you may not want to leave the Dragoons, either. But you'll have to — there's a 14-day stay limit. Saguaros, yucca and big, shady oaks are the dominant foliage. Although they're pretty, it's the rocks that are most likely to capture your attention. They balance as hoodoos and jut against the sky, making it easy to see why Cochise hid in their shadows.

The short Stronghold Nature Trail meanders around the campground and along yuccas that populate the area, while the much more difficult Cochise Trail ventures into Stronghold Canyon West. There is no water available at the campground, so you'll want to pack plenty of your own — far more than you think you'll need. While Cochise was able to survive in the Dragoons, you'll appreciate modern amenities, such as coolers chock-full of water and snacks.

ELEVATION: 5,000 feet

DIRECTIONS: From Tucson, travel east on Interstate 10 for 72 miles to U.S. Route 191 and turn right. Continue on U.S. 191 for 12 miles to Ironwood Road and turn right. Follow Ironwood Road (Forest Road 84) for about 8 miles to the campground.

INFORMATION: Douglas Ranger District, Coronado National Forest, 520-364-3468 or www.fs.usda.gov/coronado

SEASON: September through May

FEE: $10 per night

RESERVATIONS: No

AMENITIES: 🚻 🐕

CAMPFIRE TALE: Cochise Head, a rock formation in the Chiricahua Mountain Range, resembles the head (in profile) of the Apache leader.

72 | General Hitchcock Campground
Coronado National Forest, Tucson

When the Aspen Fire consumed parts of Mount Lemmon in 2003, it didn't spare picnic areas or campgrounds. Today, signs at General Hitchcock Campground warn of wildfire damage and the potential for flash foods, falling trees, and loose and rolling rocks. But while the campground has its dangers, it's also one of the finest in the area.

Small but beautiful, General Hitchcock features bountiful trees, boulder-lined campsites and big rocks to scramble up and lounge on. Green Mountain Trail originates or ends here, depending on which way you look at it, and, after a heavy rain or a particularly wet and snowy winter, Bear Creek runs through the campground.

Pine trees and picnic tables — there are plenty of both. Protect them by extinguishing your campfire completely.

ELEVATION: 6,000 feet

Sycamores and other trees and shrubs provide shelter for a variety of birds at Bog Springs Campground. 📷 RANDY PRENTICE

The Dragoon Mountains of Southeastern Arizona were once
a stronghold of Chiricahua Apaches. 📷 RANDY PRENTICE

DIRECTIONS: From Tucson, travel north on the Catalina Highway for 16.5
miles to the campground, which will be on your right.

INFORMATION: Santa Catalina Ranger District, Coronado National Forest,
520-749-8700 or www.fs.usda.gov/coronado

SEASON: Year-round

FEE: None

RESERVATIONS: No

AMENITIES:

CAMPFIRE TALE: The 3.6-mile Green Mountain Trail runs between
General Hitchcock Campground and San Pedro Vista. Categorized as
moderately difficult, the trail climbs roughly 1,300 feet.

73 | Gordon Hirabayashi Campground
Coronado National Forest, Tucson

Gordon Hirabayashi Campground used to be a prison camp. It's true.
In 1943, sociologist and activist Gordon Hirabayashi, who opposed the

internment of Japanese Americans, was sentenced to 90 days of hard labor in Catalina Honor Camp for openly defying internment and breaking curfew. In 1987, the U.S. Supreme Court overturned Hirabayashi's conviction, and in 1999, the Forest Service renamed the camp in his honor. No outright evidence of the prison camp exists today.

But, the campground is primitive. Scorched oak trees, alligator junipers, mesquites, catclaw and cottonwoods provide shade, and a gravel road runs throughout the campground.

At roughly 5,000 feet, the campground features nice views of Molino Canyon, as well as the city of Tucson to the south. A horse corral is available on-site, and the Arizona Trail passes through the campground.

ELEVATION: 5,000 feet

INFORMATION: Santa Catalina Ranger District, Coronado National Forest, 520-749-8700 or www.fs.usda.gov/coronado

DIRECTIONS: From Tucson, travel north on the Catalina Highway for 11.2 miles to the campground, which will be on your left.

SEASON: Year-round

FEE: $10 per night

RESERVATIONS: No

AMENITIES:

CAMPFIRE TALE: Prisoners built much of the Catalina Highway. Beginning in 1937, Catalina Honor Camp, which had no fences or guard towers, housed the prisoners, and after two decades, they had completed 24 miles of road through the Coronado National Forest.

Herb Martyr Campground
Coronado National Forest, Portal

Wildflowers bloom along Cave Creek, and birds flit in and out of the canyon the creek runs through. After rain, water cascades over Winn Falls — pouring from Sanders Peak — and several other nameless falls sparkle beneath them.

Herb Martyr Campground is at the end of the road that leads to the canyon, but it's divided into two separate areas. One campsite is accessible from the upper parking area, and six sites are near the lower parking area. Oaks and other hardwoods provide shade while hiking trails — Herb Martyr and Ash Spring — provide recreational opportunities for campers. Herb Martyr Trail leads to the Snowshed and Crest trails, which run deeper into the wilderness.

You get the idea. Herb Martyr is small, scenic and shady. Sure, it's a trek — to get to Portal from Tucson requires crossing the Arizona-New Mexico border — but the reward is well worth the journey.

ELEVATION: 5,800 feet

DIRECTIONS: From Portal, travel west on Forest Road 42 for about 5 miles to Forest Road 42A and turn left. Continue on FR 42A for 2 miles to the campground. FR 42A is unpaved but suitable for sedans.

INFORMATION: Douglas Ranger District, Coronado National Forest, 520-364-3468 or www.fs.usda.gov/coronado

SEASON: Year-round

FEE: None

RESERVATIONS: No

AMENITIES:

CAMPFIRE TALE: Herb Martyr Campground was named for Herb Martyr, who died during construction of a dam along Cave Creek in 1935. Today, the dam is filled in with natural debris.

75 Kartchner Caverns Campground
Kartchner Caverns State Park, Benson

If you're into stalagmites and stalactites, darkness and the occasional bat, Kartchner Caverns is for you. But beyond the supreme coolness of its caves, the state park also features a cool campground.

Just 8 miles off Interstate 10, near the Southern Arizona town of Benson, Kartchner Caverns Campground isn't a remote destination by any means. It is, of course, just outside of the caverns, where guided tours lead you underground and into the stunning limestone cathedral. Although the caverns are the obvious draw, the campground is nothing to shake a stick at.

Scrub and small trees shade the large, electric sites. Sweeping mountain views prevail, and it's possible to see the Dragoons to the east and the Huachucas to the south. In addition to the caverns, the park's recreation includes hiking, picnicking and taking photographs — the saguaros are hard to resist.

ELEVATION: 4,700 feet

DIRECTIONS: From Benson, travel west on Interstate 10 for 1.5 miles to State Route 90. Travel south on SR 90 for about 8 miles to the park.

INFORMATION: Kartchner Caverns State Park, 520-586-4100 or www.azstateparks.com/parks/kaca

SEASON: Year-round

FEE: $25 per night, plus a $6 park entrance fee

RESERVATIONS: Yes, 520-586-2283

AMENITIES:

CAMPFIRE TALE: Kartchner Caverns is home to one of the world's longest soda straw stalactites. It hangs from the ceiling of the "Throne Room" and measures more than 21 feet long.

Visitors to Lakeview Campground, at Parker Canyon Lake, enjoy plenty of water recreation, as well as views of the Canelo Hills. ◻ KEITH WHITNEY

6 | Lakeview Campground
Coronado National Forest, Sonoita

Lakeview Campground overlooks Parker Canyon Lake, and the views are spectacular — both of the water and the surrounding Canelo Hills.

Regardless of the simplicity of its name, Lakeview is an extraordinary campground. Water recreation and hiking are big draws, and a 5-mile lakefront trail features interpretive signs and fantastic opportunities to spot wildlife, including Coues deer, ospreys and, if you're lucky, bald eagles and coatis, raccoon-like creatures that have a masked face and long tail and snout.

The campground is large, with 65 sites, but it's not overwhelming. Picnic tables, fire pits and grills are among the amenities. Avid boaters will be more excited about the pier, boat ramps and docks, all within a hop, skip and a jump of the campground.

ELEVATION: 5,400 feet

DIRECTIONS: From Sonoita, travel south on State Route 83 for 25 miles to the campground, at Parker Canyon Lake.

INFORMATION: Sierra Vista Ranger District, Coronado National Forest,

520-378-0311 or www.fs.usda.gov/coronado

SEASON: Year-round

FEE: $10 per night

RESERVATIONS: No

AMENITIES: 🚻 🐕 🗑

CAMPFIRE TALE: Three Arizona State Record fish have come from Parker Canyon Lake — a 32.4-pound, 38.75-inch channel catfish; a 1.9-pound, 11-inch green sunfish; and a 2.6-pound, 16.5-inch bullhead catfish.

77 | Molino Basin Campground
Coronado National Forest, Tucson

If you're lucky, you'll meet Forest Service volunteer Richard Messinger when you visit Molino Basin. He'll tell you which are the nicest campsites — Nos. 22 through 25, in his humble opinion, but 23 has the most shade — and he'll point out the restrooms. Don't be surprised if he tells you they're the cleanest in the region. "I've got the cleanest vault toilets you'll ever find," Messinger says. "Housewives say mine are cleaner and nicer than their own."

Toilets aside, the campground itself is nice, too. Saguaros anchor the distant scenery, while manzanitas and scrub oaks are the foliage of choice on-site. The Arizona Trail runs right through the campground, and to the south are sweeping views of Tucson.

Bear-proof containers and warnings are abundant, and it's easy to see why bears are drawn to this campground. A creek trickles through, and several of the sites are right along its banks. They're accessible over a charming little footbridge. This is a place you'll want to return to — just remember to thank Mr. Messinger on your way out.

ELEVATION: 4,500 feet

DIRECTIONS: From Tucson, travel north on the Catalina Highway for 10.2 miles to the campground.

INFORMATION: Santa Catalina Ranger District, Coronado National Forest, 520-749-8700 or www.fs.usda.gov/coronado

SEASON: November through April

FEE: $10 per night

RESERVATIONS: No

AMENITIES: 🚻 🐕

Patagonia Lake has a no-wake zone for quiet paddling and fishing, and another area for speedboats. 📷 GEORGE STOCKING

Pusch Ridge Wilderness, near Molino Basin, is home to black bears, coatis and a variety of birds. The specially designated Bighorn Sheep Management Area also is within the wilderness.

Patagonia Lake Campground
Patagonia Lake State Park, Patagonia

Great blue herons love Patagonia Lake. And why wouldn't they? Its cool blue waters are full of catfish, crappie, bluegill and bass. The fish draw anglers to the lake, as well, and it's also a great place to camp.

Beaches, picnic areas, ramadas and a playground make the park family-friendly, and all-electric sites attract RV enthusiasts. Tent camping along the lake is a definite draw, and the campground is particularly popular on weekends.

As at all state parks, camping at Patagonia Lake isn't primitive. Flush toilets, showers, boat ramps and a market are but a few of the many amenities. What's more, it's a short drive to Sonoita's restaurants and shops — a getaway without having to get too far away.

ELEVATION: 3,750 feet

DIRECTIONS: Patagonia Lake State Park is at 400 Patagonia Lake Road in Patagonia.

INFORMATION: Patagonia Lake State Park, 520-287-6965 or www.azstateparks.com/parks/pala

SEASON: Year-round

FEE: $25 per night, plus a $10 park entrance fee

RESERVATIONS: Yes, 520-586-2283

AMENITIES:

Patagonia Lake State Park was established in 1975 with the 265-acre, man-made lake as its centerpiece.

Peppersauce Campground
Coronado National Forest, Oracle

If you think you'll be able to access Peppersauce Campground in late winter or early spring, you'll be mistaken. You'll venture all the way to Oracle, try to turn onto the Mount Lemmon control road that leads to Peppersauce and be greeted by a blanket of snow and a little voice

Rolling hills and desert plants, like agave, characterize the Santa Catalina Mountains, host to a number of campgrounds in this chapter. 📷 RANDY PRENTICE

inside your head saying, "Don't go there."

Consider yourself warned, then add Peppersauce Campground to your list of places to visit in late spring or summer. Broad Arizona sycamores and a variety of hardwoods line Peppersauce Creek, which usually runs dry. When it rains, though, the creek is prone to flooding, so use your judgment and steer clear during wet weather.

The campground features one large group site and 17 individual sites, all with the usual amenities. Because it's at the base of Mount Lemmon, the campground is a good hub for a scenic drive up to Cookie Cabin in Summerhaven at the mountain's summit, or for a hike or bike ride along one of the many trails. Take advantage of it all — just check the weather report before you head out.

ELEVATION: 4,700 feet

DIRECTIONS: From State Route 77 in Oracle, travel 4 miles to Forest Road 38 and turn right. Continue on FR 38 for 8 miles to the campground. The road is unpaved but passable in a sedan in the absence of rain or snow. A high-clearance, 4-wheel-drive vehicle is recommended for the drive from the campground up to Mount Lemmon.

INFORMATION: Santa Catalina Ranger District, Coronado National Forest, 520-749-8700 or www.fs.usda.gov/coronado

SEASON: Year-round

FEE: $10 per night

RESERVATIONS: No

AMENITIES: 🚻 🐾 🗑️

CAMPFIRE TALE: **Peppersauce Canyon was named by a prospector, Alex McKay, who claimed that his hot sauce went missing while he was camping in the area.**

80 | Picacho Peak Campground
Picacho Peak State Park, Picacho

As the site of the only Civil War battle in Arizona, Picacho Peak is full of history, but it's also home to one heck of a campground. Each site is electric and RV-friendly, and tent camping is also popular, thanks to shady ramadas, spacious, modern facilities, and gorgeous views of the saguaro-flanked peak. In spring, you'll see stellar sprinklings of wildflowers.

Hiking, picnicking and geocaching are among popular activities. For the little ones, there's a playground. And a visitors center is stocked with books, maps, caps, T-shirts and snacks, and volunteers eager to help.

Seasonally, the park offers guided nature walks and other ranger-led events. But the most-talked-about affair every March is "Civil War in the Southwest," a reenactment of Arizona's Civil War battle. More than 200 reenactors descend on the park, wearing authentic Civil War garb and equipped with genuine 1860s camping gear. Don't worry, though. You won't be turned away at the gate if you pack your REI goods.

ELEVATION: 2,000 feet

DIRECTIONS: Picacho Peak Campground is off Exit 219 on Interstate 10, in Picacho Peak State Park.

INFORMATION: Picacho Peak State Park, 520-466-3138 or www.azstate parks.com/parks/pipe

SEASON: Mid-September through mid-May

FEE: $25 per night, plus a $7 park entrance fee

RESERVATIONS: Yes, 520-586-2283

AMENITIES:

CAMPFIRE TALE: The Battle of Picacho Peak, sometimes referred to as the Battle of Picacho Pass, occurred April 15, 1862. The western-most skirmish of the Civil War, it was fought between a Union cavalry patrol from California and Confederate pickets from near Tucson.

Pinery Canyon Campground
Coronado National Forest, Sunizona

This small, rustic campground has a mighty view. Situated along the road that divides the Chiricahuas between Cave Creek Canyon and Chiricahua National Monument, it is home to only four campsites, and they are virtually right on top of each other.

Enormous pine trees provide shade, and amenities include toilets, fire pits and grills, but that's about it. There are none of the showers or play-grounds you'll find at the state park campgrounds in this chapter.

Really, nature is your playground here. Several trails, including Ida Peak and Pinery Horsefall, are nearby, and it's possible to trek to abandoned mining claims. But if you prefer, just sit back and absorb the history that echoes off the mountainsides where Geronimo once roamed.

ELEVATION: 7,000 feet

DIRECTIONS: From Sunizona, travel northeast on State Route 181 for 28 miles to Forest Road 42 and turn right. Continue on FR 42 for 11 miles to the campground. FR 42 is a gravel road, and high-clearance vehicles are recommended.

INFORMATION: Douglas Ranger District, Coronado National Forest, 520-364-3468 or www.fs.usda.gov/coronado

SEASON: Year-round; however, snow or heavy rain may close Forest Road 42. The road is typically open April through November, weather permitting.

FEE: None

RESERVATIONS: No

AMENITIES:

In the Apache language, Geronimo loosely translates to "one who yawns."

82 | Ramsey Vista Campground
Coronado National Forest, Sierra Vista

The Beatles sang about a long and winding road, and although John Lennon and Paul McCartney didn't have Carr Canyon Road in mind when they wrote those lyrics, you might start humming the song as you make your way toward Ramsey Vista Campground.

Set amid pine trees at the top of the road, just up from Reef Townsite Campground (below), Ramsey Vista is appropriately named. The panoramic view from any of the eight sites includes Sierra Vista, the San Pedro Valley, Ramsey Peak, Carr Canyon and Carr Peak. Unlike Reef, its lower-elevation campground companion, Ramsey Vista offers little shade but lots of manzanitas.

Although burned trees dot the landscape — fires scorched Carr Peak in 1977, 1991 and 2011, when the Monument Fire swept through — the scenery and the summer temperatures won't disappoint. At about 7,500 feet, Ramsey Vista has temperatures that are some 20 degrees lower than in nearby Sierra Vista.

ELEVATION: 7,500 feet

DIRECTIONS: Travel about 8 miles south of Sierra Vista on State Route 92 to Carr Canyon Road (Forest Road 368) and turn right. Follow Carr Canyon Road for 7 miles to the campground, which is at the end of the switch-backing gravel road. A high-clearance vehicle is recommended.

INFORMATION: Sierra Vista Ranger District, Coronado National Forest, 520-378-0311 or www.fs.usda.gov/coronado

SEASON: April through October

FEE: $10 per night

RESERVATIONS: No

AMENITIES:

Carr Peak Trail 107 originates near the parking area for Ramsey Vista Campground. It climbs 2,000 feet to the summit of Carr Peak, meandering through the burn area and along regrowth.

83 | Reef Townsite Campground
Coronado National Forest, Sierra Vista

Just a half-mile shy of Ramsey Vista Campground (No. 82), Reef seems a world away when it comes to shade. It has more pine trees, as well as

Fishing draws many visitors to Rose Canyon Lake Campground in the Santa Catalina Mountains near Tucson. 📷 EDWARD McCAIN

the manzanita that covers Ramsey Vista. Add alligator junipers, and you have a cool, wooded wonderland.

The scent of pine permeates Reef Townsite Campground, which was once the site of a quartzite-mining operation. The outpost's water system is still visible, and a short interpretive trail reveals old digs and an ore-mill foundation. For more adventurous hikers, the Old Sawmill trailhead is just across from the campground. It intersects with Miller Trail, which leads to Miller Peak. These trails were restored after the 2011 Monument Fire.

Amenities are a toilet, fire pits, grills and several shady spots to picnic, including a ramada. Be bear-aware in this area.

ELEVATION: 7,400 feet

DIRECTIONS: Travel 8 miles south of Sierra Vista on State Route 92 to Carr Canyon Road (Forest Road 368) and turn right. Follow Carr Canyon Road for 7 miles to the campground, which is at the end of the switch-backing gravel road. A high-clearance vehicle is recommended.

INFORMATION: Sierra Vista Ranger District, Coronado National Forest, 520-378-0311 or www.fs.usda.gov/coronado

SEASON: April through October

FEE: $10 per night
RESERVATIONS: No
AMENITIES: 🚻 ⛺ 🗑️

CAMPFIRE TALE: The Civilian Conservation Corps built Carr Canyon Road in the 1930s to provide access to the gold, silver and quartzite deposits on Carr Peak.

84 | Rose Canyon Campground
Coronado National Forest, Tucson

Rose Canyon Campground has one of the prettiest names in this book, and it's well deserved. On the banks of both Rose Creek and Rose Canyon Lake, the campground is a riparian oasis, especially after heavy rain.

Popular among anglers, it features 74 individual sites and two group areas. It's big, but not so big that a true outdoors experience gets lost in a sea of RVs and pavement. Trout are prevalent in the lake, which lures a variety of bird species. Bring your binoculars and while away the afternoon with a little bird-watching. Take a walk through the woods. Sit lakeside with a book.

No matter what you do, you'll want to keep coming back to Rose Canyon Campground — partly for its proximity to Tucson, partly for its beauty.

ELEVATION: 7,000 feet
DIRECTIONS: From Tucson, travel north on the Catalina Highway for 18 miles to the campground.
INFORMATION: Santa Catalina Ranger District, Coronado National Forest, 520-749-8700 or www.fs.usda.gov/coronado
SEASON: Year-round
FEE: $18 per night
RESERVATIONS: Yes
AMENITIES: 🚻 ⛺ 🗑️

CAMPFIRE TALE: The 6-acre Rose Canyon Lake is the only lake in the Santa Catalina Ranger District that is managed for recreational fishing.

85 | Rustler Park Campground
Coronado National Forest, Sunizona

If you like wildflowers, you'll love Rustler Park Campground. It's basically a meadow, and after a rainy winter, the flowers — daisies primarily — bloom with vigor. The vegetation draws a variety of wildlife, including

Coues deer and black bears, and makes for a stunning backdrop to your camping adventure.

The campground has 25 sites perched atop soft, bough-strewn earth and under the Douglas firs that line the meadow. Like its nearby counterpart, Pinery Canyon Campground (page 135), Rustler Park also affords incredible views of the Chiricahua Mountains.

Hiking is popular here, and Crest Trail is on the outskirts of the campground. At 8,500 feet, you'll want to dress in layers. It can be cold at Rustler Park, even as you're trekking the few miles on the trail to Sentinel Peak.

ELEVATION: 8,500 feet

DIRECTIONS: From Sunizona, travel northeast on State Route 181 for 28 miles to Forest Road 42 and turn right. Continue on FR 42 for about 12 miles to the campground to Forest Road 42D (at Onion Saddle). Turn right, and it's 2.5 miles to the campground. FR 42 and 42D are gravel roads, and high-clearance vehicles are recommended.

INFORMATION: Douglas Ranger District, Coronado National Forest, 520-364-3468 or www.fs.usda.gov/coronado

SEASON: April through November, weather permitting

FEE: $10 per night

RESERVATIONS: No

AMENITIES: 🚻 🐕

CAMPFIRE TALE: Rustler Park is named for the rustlers who hid stolen livestock in the area at the turn of the 20th century.

Sunny Flat Campground
Coronado National Forest, Portal

Sunny Flat will make you smile — not just because of its happy name but also because of its gorgeous setting. Near Cave Creek and situated along a meadow and amid stands of oaks and sycamores, the campground is a scenic beauty.

The rocks that loom along the creek and the water draw birds. In turn, you'll be drawn to the birds. Pack your binoculars. Just as at Bog Springs Campground (see page 123), the elegant trogon is a frequent visitor.

Sunny Flat features 14 sites, as well as picnic tables and fire pits. Unlike other campgrounds in the area, Sunny Flat has potable water during the peak season, from April through November.

Sunny Flat is also near the Chiricahua Wilderness, a swath of land known for its recreational opportunities.

ELEVATION: 5,200 feet

DIRECTIONS: From Portal, travel west on Forest Road 42 for about 3 miles to the campground.

INFORMATION: Douglas Ranger District, Coronado National Forest, 520-364-3468 or www.fs.usda.gov/coronado
SEASON: Year-round
FEE: $10 per night
RESERVATIONS: No
AMENITIES:

CAMPFIRE TALE: When you're in this neck of the woods, the Forest Service recommends taking the Cave Creek Canyon/Portal-to-Paradise scenic drive. The 17-mile loop shows off the amazing cliffs of Cave Creek Canyon.

37 | Sycamore Campground
Coronado National Forest, Sunizona

This rustic campground is shaded by — you guessed it — sycamore trees. Tucked along the banks of West Turkey Creek, Sycamore is small, with only five sites. But from the creek to the trees to the views of the Chiricahuas, its scenery packs a punch. The campground is also a good home base for adventures into the Chiricahua Wilderness, a nearly 90,000-acre playground for hikers, bikers, equestrians and history buffs. Drinking water is not available here. Nor are garbage cans, so you'll need to pack out what you pack in.

And pack your camera. Despite its smallness, Sycamore is stunning.

ELEVATION: 6,200 feet
DIRECTIONS: From Sunizona, travel east on State Route 181 for 14 miles to Forest Road 41 and continue east. Follow FR 41 for 9 miles to the campground. A high-clearance vehicle is recommended. Do not attempt to traverse FR 41 after a rainstorm.
INFORMATION: Douglas Ranger District, Coronado National Forest, 520-364-3468 or www.fs.usda.gov/coronado
SEASON: Year-round
FEE: None
RESERVATIONS: No
AMENITIES:

CAMPFIRE TALE: North American sycamores are divided into three distinct subcategories: American sycamores (*Platanus occidentalis*), California or Western sycamores (*Platanus racemosa*), and Arizona sycamores (*Platanus wrightii*).

Cathedral Point, one of the many unique rock formations in the Chiricahua Mountains, towers over Sunny Flat Campground. ■ RANDY PRENTICE

Buckskin Mountain State Park
📷 PAUL GILL

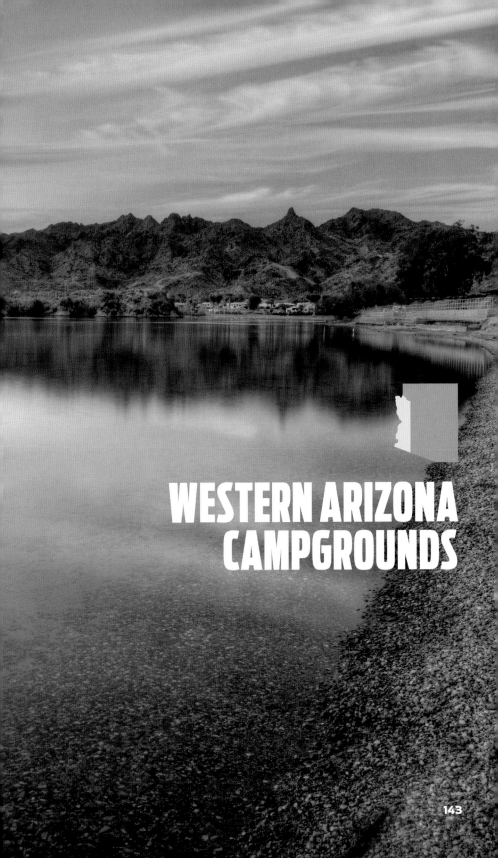

WESTERN ARIZONA CAMPGROUNDS

When most people
think of the West
Coast, they think
of Los Angeles, San Diego
and other beachfront California towns. But we have
a "West Coast" of our own
here in Arizona. Camp-
grounds are nestled along
the Colorado River, in towns
like Parker and Lake Havasu
City and north of Yuma. Still
more are in places a little
more inland, like at Hualapai
Mountain Park, outside of
Kingman. Of course, boat-
ing and fishing are the draws
along the "coast," but if
you're into a side of hiking
with your camping experi-
ence, Western Arizona
won't disappoint.

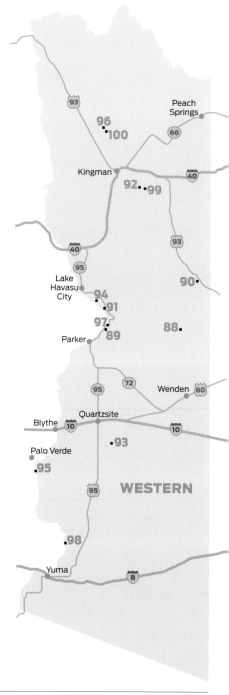

Alamo Lake Campground
Alamo Lake State Park, Wenden

People go to Alamo Lake State Park to look at the stars. As a member of the Global Star Network, it's recognized for its public stargazing events and dedication to maintaining dark skies and educating the public about astronomy.

While you're here for a star party, you might as well stay at the park's campground. In Bill Williams River Valley, away from big city lights, it's the perfect place to pick out constellations. Right on the banks of Alamo Lake, it's also a prime destination for anglers looking to snag crappie, catfish, bass and bluegill.

As are all state park campgrounds, Alamo Lake is well developed and features extra amenities like showers, a visitors center and a gift shop. RVs frequent the campground, but tent campers will appreciate lakeside sites and, of course, the inky night skies.

ELEVATION: 1,300 feet

DIRECTIONS: From Wenden, travel north on Alamo Road for 28 miles to Wickenburg Road and turn left. Follow Wickenburg Road for about 5 miles to Alamo Lake State Park.

INFORMATION: Alamo Lake State Park, 928-669-2088 or www.azstate parks.com/parks/alla

SEASON: Year-round

FEE: $13–$25 per night, plus a $7 park-entrance fee

RESERVATIONS: Yes, 520-586-2283

AMENITIES:

CAMPFIRE TALE: Completion of the Alamo Dam in 1968 resulted in Alamo Lake. It's on the Bill Williams River, where the Big Sandy and Santa Maria rivers converge.

Buckskin Mountain Campground
Buckskin Mountain State Park, Parker

Warning: If you're looking for remote, off-the-beaten-path, into-the-wild camping, don't read this entry. Buckskin Mountain Campground isn't rustic by any stretch of the imagination.

It is, however, a haven for families. Kids love it because of its water recreation, playground and arcade. Moms love it because of its grocery store and restaurant. Dads love it because of its on-site gas station.

The campground is along the Colorado River, and boating, fishing and Jet-skiing are popular activities. The road through the campground is paved, and sites are fairly spacious. Because the campground is within a state park, it's RV-friendly, but tent campers will enjoy the wind off the

water and spacious sites.

ELEVATION: 420 feet

DIRECTIONS: From Parker, travel north on State Route 95 for about 12 miles to Buckskin Mountain State Park.

INFORMATION: Buckskin Mountain State Park, 928-667-3231 or www.azstateparks.com/parks/bumo

SEASON: Year-round

FEE: $25–$28 per night, plus a $10 park-entrance fee

RESERVATIONS: Yes, 520-586-2283

AMENITIES:

CAMPFIRE TALE: Parker Dam, the world's deepest dam at 320 feet, is 5 miles north of Buckskin Mountain Campground.

90 | Burro Creek Campground
Burro Creek Recreation Site, Kingman

Tucked along the riparian area created by Burro Creek, this campground might at first seem to be a mirage. The green of the creek-fed trees and shrubs glows against a dusty desert background, and the creek, when it runs, blazes blue.

Wildflowers bloom in spring, and the Bureau of Land Management tends an interpretive cactus garden. Sweeping views of Burro Creek Bridge and the surrounding saguaro-studded hillsides abound.

Amenities are also surprising. Each site is equipped with a picnic table, a grill, a ramada and a parking space. Drinking water is available, and restrooms include flush toilets and sinks.

ELEVATION: 1,900 feet

DIRECTIONS: From Kingman, travel east on Interstate 40 for 17 miles to U.S. Route 93. Travel south on U.S. 93 for 53 miles to the campground turnoff, 1 mile south of Burro Creek Bridge.

INFORMATION: Kingman Field Office, Bureau of Land Management, 928-718-3700 or www.blm.gov/az

SEASON: Year-round

FEE: $14 per night

RESERVATIONS: No

AMENITIES:

CAMPFIRE TALE: Upper Burro Creek Wilderness Area is home to more than 150 bird species, including falcons and buzzards.

Cattail Cove State Park features a swimming area and boat dock, in addition to views of the Whipple Mountains. KERRICK JAMES

01 Cattail Cove Campground
Cattail Cove State Park, Lake Havasu City

Of the 61 campsites at Cattail Cove State Park, 28 are accessible by boat only. Like other state-park campgrounds, Cattail Cove is well developed and chock-full of amenities, including a fish-cleaning station.

Campsites, with the exception of the boat-accessible sites, are situated toward the center of the park, but lake access is easy. Boats, of course, are welcome, and there's plenty of room for them. The same goes for RVs, which are popular here because of electrical hookups and a dump station.

Rockhounds are fond of this campground and the Lake Havasu area in general — agate, obsidian, turquoise and geodes are abundant in the rocky landscape.

ELEVATION: 450 feet

DIRECTIONS: From Parker, travel north on State Route 95 for 24 miles to Cattail Cove State Park.

INFORMATION: Cattail Cove State Park, 928-855-1223 or www.azstate parks.com/parks/caco

SEASON: Year-round

FEE: $15–$26 per night, plus a $10–$15 park-entrance fee

RESERVATIONS: Yes, 520-586-2283

AMENITIES:

CAMPFIRE TALE: Lake Havasu was formed when the Colorado River was dammed near Parker. It is home to dozens of fish species, including bluegill, catfish, crappie and bass.

02 Hualapai Mountain Campground
Hualapai Mountain Park, Kingman

Camping comes in many forms at Hualapai Mountain Park — from cabins that sleep 12 to mountaintop RV sites to teepees. Yes, you can camp in a teepee. And if you have kids, it's something you should do at least once. Just think of the photo potential.

There are 19 cabins, 11 RV-friendly spots and more than 70 standard campsites. The Civilian Conservation Corps built the 2,300-acre park in the 1930s. It's in a gorgeous mountain setting just outside of Kingman, and because of its cool weather and adventure-friendly terrain, it's a great place to hike or bike or just sit around and wait for wildlife.

The Aspen Peak Trail originates from Hualapai Mountain Park, near Kingman. 📷 ELIAS BUTLER

In fact, 10 miles of trail run through the park, including Aspen Peak Trail, which leads to the top of its namesake and amazing views of mountains and Kingman. Back at the teepee, enjoy the semirustic camping experience, the shade provided by oaks, and the strong, sharp scent of pines.

ELEVATION: 5,000 feet

DIRECTIONS: From Kingman, travel east on Interstate 40 for 6 miles to Exit 59. From there, travel south on DW Ranch Road for 4.5 miles to Hualapai Mountain Road and turn left. Continue on Hualapai Mountain Road for 4 miles to the park's ranger station.

INFORMATION: Hualapai Mountain Park, 928-681-5700 or www.mcparks.com

SEASON: Year-round

FEE: $15 per night for dry camping; $25 for RVs; $35 for teepees; cabin rates vary depending on day and size of cabin, from $50 to $125 per night.

RESERVATIONS: Yes, 928-681-5700

AMENITIES:

CAMPFIRE TALE: *Hualapai* **translates to "Pine tree folk" in the language of the Indian tribe of the same name.**

93 | Kofa National Wildlife Refuge
Yuma and Quartzsite

For a few reasons, this destination is different from any other in this book. First, there's no designated campground. Second, it's the only national wildlife refuge in this guide. Third, it may be the only place you'll see rare flora and fauna.

Visitors may camp anywhere, as long as they don't do so within a quarter-mile of a watering hole, and vehicles must remain within 100 feet of designated roads. Big sky, big country and big opportunities to see animals such as foxes, desert bighorn sheep (one of the largest herds in the Southwest), deer and rabbits are the main attractions here.

A variety of plants — including the Kofa Mountain barberry, a plant found only in Southwestern Arizona — also draws botany buffs to the refuge. With more than 600,000 acres at your disposal, you're bound to find something to do. Because of the lack of designated camping areas, though, it's even more important to heed the Leave No Trace principles.

ELEVATION: Varies across the refuge. Signal Peak in the Kofa Mountains is at 4,877 feet; Castle Dome Peak in the Castle Dome Mountains is at 3,788 feet.

DIRECTIONS: From Yuma, travel north on U.S. Route 95 for 40 miles to the refuge.

INFORMATION: Kofa National Wildlife Refuge, 928-783-7861 or www.fws.gov

SEASON: November through April

Last light paints teddy bear chollas in the Kofa National Wildlife Refuge. GEORGE STOCKING

FEE: None

RESERVATIONS: No

AMENITIES: 👫 🗑

CAMPFIRE TALE: Arizona's only native palm trees grow in Palm Canyon, a highlight of Kofa National Wildlife Refuge. Fewer than 100 are left. They are visible from Palm Canyon Trail, a National Recreational Trail from which you also might spot desert bighorn sheep.

4 | Lake Havasu Campground
Lake Havasu State Park, Lake Havasu City

Forty-seven lakefront campsites dot the landscape at Lake Havasu State Park, where camping comes with built-in entertainment courtesy of the lake, which beckons boaters, anglers, personal watercraft users and beach loungers with its cool blue waters and view of the famous London Bridge. A trail runs along the shoreline for visitors who prefer a side of terrestrial endeavors to go along with their aquatic ones.

The road around the campground is paved, and each site is shady and somewhat spacious. An interpretive garden is well cared for by the park's staff, and rabbits, lizards, raptors and water-loving birds are common sights — as are snowbirds, who flock to Lake Havasu City for a little fun in the sun.

ELEVATION: 480 feet

DIRECTIONS: Lake Havasu State Park is at 699 London Bridge Road in Lake Havasu.

INFORMATION: Lake Havasu State Park, 928-855-2784 or www. azstate parks.com/parks/laha

SEASON: Year-round

FEE: $18 per night

RESERVATIONS: Yes, 520-586-2283

AMENITIES:

CAMPFIRE TALE: In 1968, American entrepreneur Robert P. McCulloch purchased the London Bridge for $2.46 million. He had it dismantled and moved to Lake Havasu City, where it was rebuilt and rededicated in 1971.

95 | Oxbow Campground
Bureau of Land Management, Yuma

There are no designated sites at Oxbow Campground, some 68 miles northwest of Yuma and along the Colorado River, but locations on an oxbow of the Colorado go the quickest.

That's a no-brainer, considering the lure of the Colorado and the promise of water recreation. Hiking, boating and swimming are popular activities, and Oxbow is also adjacent to Cibola National Wildlife Refuge. Part of Oxbow is across the state line, in California.

If you're camping here for more than a day, take a trip to the refuge, which has more than 288 bird species and Sonoran Desert standouts including coyotes, desert tortoises and mule deer. Back at the campground, you might spot even more wildlife, especially deer.

ELEVATION: 140 feet

DIRECTIONS: From Yuma, travel west on Interstate 8 and into California. From the state line, continue west on I-8 to Ogilby Road. Travel north on Ogilby Road for 24 miles to California State Route 78. Travel north on CSR 78 for 26 miles to signs for Cibola Wildlife Refuge. Turn east at the gravel road and continue for 0.5 miles to the campground. An alternate route from Blythe, California, is available on the BLM website.

INFORMATION: Yuma Field Office, Bureau of Land Management, 928-317-3200 or www.blm.gov

SEASON: November through April

FEE: $15 per night

RESERVATIONS: No

AMENITIES:

CAMPFIRE TALE: Yuma was first incorporated as Arizona City in

1871. Today, it's the largest city in Yuma County, and had 93,000 people in the 2011 Census, nearly half the county's population.

6 Packsaddle Campground
Bureau of Land Management, Chloride

Chloride bills itself as "an old mining camp that never quite died." With a population of about 250, it operates as a living ghost town of sorts, attracting visitors with Roy Purcell murals and the promise of ghost-miner sightings.

Whether ghost-miners exist is for you to decide. And because Packsaddle Campground is perched in the Cerbat Mountains, just above Chloride, chances are you'll have an opportunity to seek answers to the paranormal mystery.

The campground features big scenery and plenty of shade, and at an elevation of 6,000 feet, it's cooler than the towns on the desert floor below. Piñon pines, junipers and standard campground amenities make Packsaddle a pleasant destination.

ELEVATION: 6,000 feet

DIRECTIONS: From Kingman, travel north on U.S. Route 93 for 18 miles to Big Wash Road and turn right. Follow Big Wash Road for 9 miles to the campground. A high-clearance vehicle is recommended. The BLM advises against vehicles with travel trailers on Big Wash Road.

INFORMATION: Kingman Field Office, Bureau of Land Management, 928-718-3700 or www.blm.gov

SEASON: Year-round

FEE: None

RESERVATIONS: No

AMENITIES: 🚻 🐕

CAMPFIRE TALE: Cherum Peak Trail originates about 12 miles up Big Wash Road. The 5.4-mile round-trip hike climbs 1,000 feet to the top of its namesake peak.

07 River Island Campground
River Island State Park, Parker

Sometimes, particularly during summer, people who live in Arizona's desert regions lament their landlocked status. They yearn for water. That's why so many people flock west to the beaches of San Diego.

But Arizona's "West Coast" also has a lot to offer, particularly at River Island State Park, where beachfront campsites go a long way toward shaking the summer blues. With 37 sites, a boat dock, a beach, a cove and picnic areas, the park is an easy getaway.

Personal watercraft and swimming are popular, as is daydreaming. The water and surrounding mountains can do that to a person, so don't be surprised if you find yourself drifting off for a bit.

ELEVATION: 420 feet

DIRECTIONS: From Parker, travel north on State Route 95 for 12 miles to River Island State Park.

INFORMATION: River Island State Park, 928-667-3386 or www.azstate parks.com/parks/riis

SEASON: Year-round

FEE: $25 per night, plus a $10 park-entry fee

RESERVATIONS: Yes, 520-586-2283

AMENITIES:

CAMPFIRE TALE: Arizona is home to 28 state parks and three state natural areas, from River Island and Catalina to Red Rock and Tubac Presidio and more.

98 | Squaw Lake Campground
Bureau of Land Management, Yuma

With 125 RV sites, Squaw Lake Campground is popular. Tent campers shouldn't be deterred, though, as tent sites are dispersed throughout.

It's one of the more developed destinations in the Bureau of Land Management's campground portfolio, thanks to boat ramps (including direct access to the Colorado River), flush toilets, designated swimming areas and picnic tables. But that's not to say that a true nature experience is lost here.

Squaw Lake draws wildlife and waterfowl, so don't be surprised to find a quail or a coyote roaming around. Plus, a hiking trail traverses the campground. Developed and down to earth, Squaw Lake is everything a car camper could ask for.

ELEVATION: 200 feet

DIRECTIONS: From Interstate 8 in Yuma, exit at Fourth Avenue to Imperial County Road. Follow Imperial County Road north for 22 miles to Senator Wash Road and turn left. Follow Senator Wash Road for 4 miles to the campground.

INFORMATION: Yuma Field Office, Bureau of Land Management, 928-317-3200 or www.blm.gov

SEASON: Year-round

FEE: $15 per night

RESERVATIONS: No

AMENITIES:

Wild Cow Springs Campground, in the Hualapai Mountains, is populated by pines and Gambel oaks. 📷 ROBERT McDONALD

CAMPFIRE TALE: Imperial Dam was constructed in 1938, 18 miles northeast of Yuma. It includes three desilting basins to remove sediment from Colorado River water to help keep canals clear.

9 | Wild Cow Springs Campground
Bureau of Land Management, Kingman

Tucked within the Hualapai Mountains, Wild Cow Springs Campground is a small, scenic wonder. At roughly 6,200 feet in elevation, the campground is cool and green, shaded by ponderosa pines and oaks.

Although the campground overlooks the dusty desert floor, you won't mind. You'll be too impressed by the location of the campground — within a short drive of Kingman — as well as by the hiking, biking and relaxing that the campground inspires. Even the drive to Wild Cow Springs is something special. The road winds along old mining claims and into the forest, and when the sky blazes bright blue, it's as if you're venturing into a hidden gem of a destination.

Amenities are minimal, but you will find a restroom, trash receptacles, picnic tables and fire rings. Just down the road is Hualapai Mountain Park, with its 10 miles of hiking trails, ranger-led programs and visitors center.

ELEVATION: 6,200 feet

DIRECTIONS: From Kingman, travel east on Interstate 40 for 6 miles to Exit 59. From there, travel south on DW Ranch Road for 4.5 miles to Hualapai Mountain Road and turn left. Continue on Hualapai Mountain Road for 14 miles to Pine Lake Fire Station, and turn right on the unmarked, one-lane

road. Follow the road for about 5 miles to Wild Cow Springs Recreation Area. A high-clearance vehicle is recommended.

INFORMATION: Kingman Field Office, Bureau of Land Management, 928-718-3700 or www.blm.gov

SEASON: May through October

FEE: $5 per night

RESERVATIONS: No

AMENITIES:

CAMPFIRE TALE: Wild Cow Springs got its name from the unbranded or escaped cattle that once roamed the area.

Windy Point Campground
Bureau of Land Management, Chloride

Just 2 miles past Packsaddle Campground, along Big Wash Road, Windy Point Campground is appropriately named. At a moderately high elevation, with sweeping views of the valley, it seems as if the wind wants to kiss the top of the Cerbat Mountains.

Bird-watching, hiking and picnicking are big here. The route to the campground is a scenic drive in and of itself, and photo opportunities abound. Amenities include picnic tables, fire pits and grills, and Chloride is a short drive away, in case you've forgotten your s'mores supplies.

Try not to forget the marshmallows. Or the firewood. None is available at the campground.

ELEVATION: 6,000 feet

DIRECTIONS: From Kingman, travel north on U.S. Route 93 for 18 miles to Big Wash Road and turn right. Follow Big Wash Road for 11 miles to the campground. A high-clearance vehicle is recommended. The BLM recommends against vehicles with travel trailers on Big Wash Road.

INFORMATION: Kingman Field Office, Bureau of Land Management, 928-718-3700 or www.blm.gov

SEASON: Year-round

FEE: $8 per night

RESERVATIONS: No

AMENITIES:

CAMPFIRE TALE: The Cerbat Mountains range for 23 miles in Northwestern Arizona. They lie directly east of the Black Mountains, and their highest point is Cherum Peak, at 6,983 feet.

Nestled in the Cerbat Mountains, Windy Point Campground overlooks Chloride. ◻ ELIAS BUTLER

Index